Paddington at Work

'Among the various animals who have been introduced into the human (fictional) world to create chaos out of order, the bear called Paddington stands very high. It is a pleasure to be able to laugh at human absurdity through the mishaps that befall this pseudo-human.'

Margery Fisher, Growing Point

'Written with a sense of humour that is alternately slyly witty or exuberantly farcical. . . . Well and amusingly illustrated by Peggy Fortnum.'

Books and Bookmen

'Within a comparatively short time, Paddington has joined Pooh as one of the great bears of children's literature.'

The Teacher

'As for Paddington, he reduced my eight-year-old research assistant to louder giggles than any of the other books.'

New Statesman

Also by Michael Bond in Lions

Michael Bond

Paddington At Work

With drawings by Peggy Fortnum

Collins · Lions

First published 1966 by William Collins Sons & Co Ltd
14 St James's Place, London sw1
First published in Lions 1975
Second Impression 1976

Printed in Great Britain
by William Collins Sons & Co Ltd
Glasgow

Contents

1.
A Bear at Sea

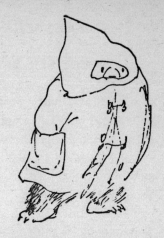

Paddington woke with a start and after blinking several times in order to accustom his eyes to the evening light, peered round the deck of the liner *Karenia* with a puzzled expression on his face.

If he hadn't known it was quite impossible, for the ship was still over two days' sailing-time away from England, let alone number thirty-two Windsor Gardens in London, he would have sworn he'd just heard his name being called, quite loudly, not only by Mr Brown, but by the rest of the family, Mrs Brown, Jonathan and Judy, not to mention Mrs Bird into the bargain.

Normally Paddington was rather keen on dreams. Some of the ones he'd had in the past had been very good value indeed, especially after one of Mrs Bird's heavy suppers. But as he looked around the deserted deck of the great ship he began to decide that the one he'd just experienced seemed almost too real for his liking.

It was that time in the day when the half-light from the setting sun plays strange tricks with the shadows, and with most of the other passengers still below and not even so much as the friendly white coat of a steward anywhere in sight, Paddington almost wished he hadn't partaken of a second helping of the suet pudding which the chef had prepared especially for him that evening.

Pausing only to dip one paw into a nearby jar of marmalade, he pulled his duffle coat hood more firmly over his head and then settled back again in the deck-chair as he turned his attention to a large tin marked OSBORNE BISCUITS — PROPERTY OF P. BROWN ESQ. WANTED ON VOYAGE, which stood near by.

Paddington liked Osborne biscuits, especially when they were covered in a thick layer of marmalade chunks, and soon a steady munching sound broke the stillness of the evening air.

The journey to Darkest Peru in order to take part in his Aunt Lucy's birthday celebrations at the Home for Retired Bears in Lima had been a long and enjoyable one, but all the same, now that he was nearing the end of the return voyage, Paddington was beginning to feel more and more excited at the prospect of seeing all his old friends once again, and after a moment's thought he put this down as the cause of his unusually lifelike dream.

Gradually the combination of a large and most enjoyable dinner, the sea air, and the distant throb of the engines far below, all had a soothing effect. In no time at all he was fast asleep again, and not even the plonk of an Osborne biscuit as it slipped from his paw and rolled across the deck towards the scuppers served to waken him.

Paddington wasn't quite sure when it happened, or how long it lasted, but suddenly he found himself in the middle of yet another dream and to his surprise it once again had to do with the Browns.

As a dream it was, if anything, even more vivid than the first one.

It all started when he dropped one of his biscuits at the top of a steep hill near Windsor Gardens. Instead of breaking or even falling over on its side, it landed edge downwards and immediately started rolling after him. Worse still, with every passing second it grew larger and larger, and as it grew larger so it rolled faster until in the end Paddington found himself running down the Portobello Road, in and out of all the market stalls, as fast as his legs would carry him.

All the time, although he couldn't see them, he could distinctly hear the voices of the Brown family calling out his name.

And then the worst happened. One moment he was running along the road mopping his brow and glancing anxiously over his shoulder at the pursuing biscuit, the next moment it was just as if he had stepped into a great pool of treacle. The more he tried to move his legs, the more impossible it became, until quite suddenly he woke with a start and found himself sitting on the deck almost completely enveloped in his duffle coat.

As he struggled free Paddington discovered to his surprise that not only had he got one of his paws stuck inside the jar of marmalade but that in his excitement he'd also knocked over the tin of biscuits and quite a number of them had rolled out on to the deck.

It was a large tin and it had been given to him by his Aunt Lucy as a parting gift just before he set sail on the return voyage to England. Even though he'd had to dip into it quite heavily on a number of occasions, there were still several layers left, and Paddington had no wish to lose any of them before the end of the journey so he spent the next few seconds hastily gathering up the remains.

It was as he picked up the last of the biscuits that

he suddenly froze in his tracks and stared along the deck at a group of five very familiar figures who had suddenly appeared out of a patch of shadow near the stern.

Before he even had time to blink the figures all began waving frantically and calling his name as they moved towards him in a body.

Pinching himself several times in order to make sure he wasn't dreaming, Paddington looked wildly about the ship for somewhere to hide and then, hastily scooping the remains of the marmalade back into the jar with one paw, he replaced the lid on his tin of Osbornes with the other and disappeared through a nearby door as fast as his legs would carry him.

A few seconds later he emerged on the other side of the ship, took one last look along the deck in case he was still being pursued, and then paused before yet another door which had a red cross over the top and the words SHIP'S DOCTOR written in large red letters on the panelling.

Paddington was a brave bear at heart and when something out of the ordinary happened he was usually only too ready to investigate the matter on his own account, but the events of the past few minutes had been altogether too impossible to explain for his liking and he was anxious to seek a second opinion on the matter.

The Ship's Doctor looked most surprised when the door opened and Paddington entered his cabin. 'Have you got an appointment, bear?' he asked briskly.

Paddington placed his belongings on the floor and put a paw to his lips as he bent down to lock the door. Because of his fur it was a bit difficult for him to actually look as white as a sheet, but there was something about the end of his nose and the way he stood that caused the Doctor to jump up from his seat in alarm.

'Good gracious!' he exclaimed. 'What on earth is the matter?'

Paddington crossed the cabin towards the Doctor and collapsed into a chair in front of the desk. 'I don't think it's anything on earth,' he replied ominously, casting an anxious glance over his shoulder.

The Doctor sat down again and eyed Paddington nervously. 'I must say,' he began, in an attempt at jollity, 'you look rather as if you've just seen a ghost.'

'I have,' said Paddington, feeling a bit better now that he'd reached the safety of the well-lit cabin. 'Five of them!'

'Five?' echoed the Doctor. 'Dear me. I think perhaps you'd better tell me all about it.'

'Well,' began Paddington, taking a deep breath. 'It happened soon after I was chased by an Osborne.'

'Soon after you were chased by a *what?*' exclaimed the Doctor.

'An Osborne biscuit,' repeated Paddington patiently.

The Doctor gave a nervous, rather high-pitched laugh. 'You're sure it wasn't a Bath Oliver or a Garibaldi?' he asked.

Paddington gave him a hard stare. 'It was an Osborne,' he said firmly as he held up his tin. 'It says so on the label. My Aunt Lucy gave them to me. It fell out of the tin and then it chased me all the way down the Portobello Road.'

The Doctor looked at Paddington and then at the cabin door, almost as if he were measuring the distance. Although they'd passed quite close to each other several times on the voyage, it was the first time they'd actually spoken, and there was something about Paddington's unwinking stare which was beginning to make him feel rather uneasy. 'You were followed all down the Portobello Road by an Osborne biscuit?' he repeated casually.

'That's right,' said Paddington, pleased that he'd got his point over at last. 'It was only a small one to start with, but it got bigger and bigger. Then I couldn't move my paws.'

'Couldn't move paws,' repeated the Doctor, busily writing it all down.

'They felt as if they had lead weights on them,' continued Paddington.

'Lead . . . weights . . .' echoed the Doctor, still writing. 'Good. I'll see what a little embrocation will do.'

'Oh, that's all right, thank you very much,' said Paddington cheerfully. 'They're better now. It was only because I'd stepped in my marmalade by mistake. I got one of my paws stuck in the jar.'

The Ship's Doctor removed his glasses, blew on them, and then stared first at Paddington's outstretched paw and then at his highly polished floor where several marmalade chunks lay where they had fallen during Paddington's hasty entrance.

'Did anything else happen after that?' he asked distastefully.

Paddington nodded. 'I saw all the Browns!' he announced impressively.

'Browns?' repeated the Doctor, not quite sure if he'd heard aright. 'No green or blues?'

Paddington gave the Doctor another even harder stare. 'Browns,' he repeated firmly. 'There were four of them. *And* Mrs Bird.'

'Mrs Bird!' exclaimed the Doctor. 'You're sure it wasn't a seagull? It may have stayed on board after we stopped at the last port. They often do.'

'A *seagull*!' exclaimed Paddington hotly. 'It was Mrs Bird. From number thirty-two Windsor Gardens. I was sitting on the deck . . .'

'Ah!' The Doctor's face cleared as if by magic. 'You've been sitting on the deck, have you?'

'Yes,' said Paddington. 'I was having a bit of a nap after dinner. And then I had a dream – only it wasn't one really.'

'All day?' asked the Doctor. 'In the sun?'

'Well, I did have a bit of a sunbathe this morning after I'd been to the baker's,' admitted Paddington. 'And then another one this afternoon.'

'You've been suffering from hallucinations, bear,' said the Doctor briskly, looking quite pleased that he'd solved the problem at last. 'I've met this sort of thing before. Too much sun and people begin to imagine all sorts of things. Though I must say I don't think I've ever come across anyone who thought they were being chased by an Osborne biscuit.'

He opened a drawer in his desk and withdrew a bottle. 'Sleep, that's what you need, bear – plenty of sleep. I'll give you some tablets to help you along.'

Paddington's face had been growing longer and longer during the Doctor's recital and at the mention of the word 'sleep' it reached its longest ever. He'd had quite enough sleep for one day even if some of the dreams had been hallucinations.

'But I did see the Browns,' he complained, looking most upset. 'And it wasn't a dream because I pinched myself. And they couldn't have been there because they're in London. So they must have been ghosts.'

'Nonsense!' exclaimed the Doctor briskly. 'There's no such thing as . . .' His voice broke off and a strange expression suddenly came over his face as he stared at something beyond Paddington's right shoulder.

He gave a gulp, rubbed his glasses again, and then gripped the edge of the table. 'Er . . . how many ghosts did you think you saw?'

'Five,' replied Paddington, running through his list.

As Paddington mentioned each name in turn the Doctor's face seemed to go an even paler shade of white until by the time he reached Mrs Bird's name all the colour had drained away.

'You did lock the door when you came in, didn't you?' he asked casually.

'I think so,' said Paddington, beginning to look worried himself at the expression on the Doctor's face. 'It's a bit difficult with paws, but . . .'

Paddington looked round and as he did so he nearly fell backwards out of his chair with surprise. For there, before his very eyes, neatly framed in a large porthole next to the door, were five very familiar faces. Not just Mr Brown, whose face, pressed hard against the glass, had taken on an unusually flat and puddingy appearance, but Mrs Brown, Jonathan, Judy, and Mrs

Bird as well.

Reaching across the table the Doctor picked up a telephone. 'Get me the Master at Arms at once, please,' he barked. 'And tell him to hurry. There's something nasty going on outside my porthole.'

'It's all right, bear,' he continued. 'There's no need to be alarmed.' Slamming the telephone receiver back on to its cradle the Ship's Doctor turned back to Paddington and then broke off in mid-speech.

He had been about to explain that help was on the way, but from the glazed expression on Paddington's face as he lay back in the chair with his paws in the air it looked very much as if one occupant of the cabin at least was beyond caring.

Mrs Brown dabbed at Paddington's forehead with some eau-de-Cologne as he sat up in his bunk and stared round the cabin.

'Thank goodness,' she exclaimed. 'We thought you were never coming round.'

'Every time you caught sight of us you fell over again,' said Judy. 'We were getting jolly worried.'

Paddington rubbed his eyes as if he could still hardly believe them. 'I thought you were a halluci-something,' he explained.

Mrs Brown turned to her husband. 'It's all your fault, Henry,' she said. 'If we'd gone to the Purser's office in the first place as I suggested all this would never have happened.'

'I wanted it to be a surprise,' complained Mr Brown. 'How was I to know Paddington would think we were all ghosts!'

Mr Brown was looking a trifle fed up. It had been his idea that the Brown family should combine their summer holiday with a trip home on Paddington's liner, meeting it at a point when it was still two days away from England.

At the time it had seemed a very good idea and when they'd boarded the liner late that afternoon at its last port of call they had all been looking forward not only to the experience but also to seeing the look on Paddington's face when they confronted him.

They hadn't bargained on his reacting in quite the way he had and Mr Brown was tending to get most of the blame.

'Well,' said Mrs Bird, 'I must say that if I thought someone was hundreds of miles away and then I suddenly met them face to face in the middle of an ocean I'd be upset.'

'And at night,' said Judy. 'I bet it was jolly frightening.'

'Besides, I don't think Paddington was the only one to be taken in,' added Jonathan. 'I don't think the Ship's Doctor was too keen on us either.'

'I've always heard sailors are supposed to be superstitious,' said Mrs Brown, surveying her husband as he helped himself to a sandwich from a pile next to Paddington's bunk, 'but you don't look much like a ghost to me, Henry.'

'I don't think the Doctor thought so when he got over the first shock,' said Judy. 'He looked jolly cross.'

The Browns' laughter was suddenly broken into by a tap on the cabin door.

'I expect that's my cocoa,' said Paddington importantly. 'The steward always brings me some before I go to bed.'

The others exchanged glances as the door opened and a man in a white coat entered carrying a tray laden with a large jug of steaming hot liquid.

'This is the life,' exclaimed Mr Brown. 'I must say I'm looking forward to the rest of the voyage. Sunshine and deck games all day. Bear's cocoa last thing at night to round things off. Even a ghost couldn't ask for more!'

Paddington nodded happily as the steward sorted out some extra mugs and began to pour. He was keen on cocoa at the best of times, especially ship's cocoa, which somehow always had a taste of its own, and now that the problem of the ghosts had been solved he was looking forward to his nightcap, particularly as it also celebrated the unexpected early meeting with the Brown family.

He eyed the jug from behind a cloud of rich, brown steam. 'There's only one thing nicer, Mr Brown,' he announced amid general agreement. 'And that's *two* cups!'

2.
Anchors Away

Mr Brown gazed along the broad deck of the *Karenia* with a puzzled look on his face. 'Has anyone noticed Paddington lately?' he asked. 'He seems to be acting very strangely.'

The rest of the family followed the direction of Mr Brown's gaze and were just in time to see a familiar figure emerge from behind a lifeboat some distance away, stand for a moment staring up at the sky with a very odd expression indeed, and then hurry back to the rail.

'He was all right at lunch time,' said Mrs Brown. 'I do hope it's nothing he's eaten.'

'Perhaps he's got something in his eye,' suggested Mrs Bird, as Paddington stepped backwards and then almost fell over as he bent himself double in order to peer up at the sky again.

'He was tapping the barometer outside the Purser's officer earlier on,' said Jonathan. 'I thought he was going to break it.'

'*And* he's got some seaweed hanging out of his porthole,' exclaimed Judy.

'It must be something to do with the weather,' said Mr Brown, turning his attention back to the ship's newspaper. 'Perhaps he think's we're going to have a storm.'

'Crikey! I hope not,' exclaimed Jonathan. 'I don't want to miss the party to-night.'

'If I know Paddington,' replied Mr Brown, 'he won't either. I expect that's why he's worried.'

Satisfied with Mr Brown's explanations, most of the family returned to their various activities. After a morning spent exploring the great ship they were only too glad to have a rest. Travelling on an ocean liner was an exciting event, not unlike being let loose in a miniature floating town, and with Paddington acting as guide, almost as tiring.

During his long voyage he'd made friends with a good many of the ship's crew, so that apart from visiting the shops, the swimming pool, the gymnasium, and various lounges, they'd also been taken on a tour of inspection of the ship's kennels, the bakery, the engine room, and many other places not normally open to the public.

The only person who wasn't quite satisfied with Mr Brown's explanation was Mrs Bird, and she wisely forbode to mention that to the best of her knowledge Paddington didn't even know there was a party taking place that evening, let alone that he was going to it.

From past experience she knew only too well that whatever it was Paddington had on his mind, matters couldn't be hurried and that all would be revealed in due course.

Unaware that he'd been arousing so much interest, Paddington dipped his paw in a nearby mug of cocoa, held it up in order to see which way the wind was blowing, and then peered anxiously over the side of the ship towards the blue waters far below.

All in all, he decided things looked much too calm for his liking.

It wasn't that he was particularly keen on rough weather. In fact, on the few occasions when the *Karenia* had been caught in a storm and he'd had to miss a meal he'd been upset in more ways than one. But for once, alone among the many hundreds of passengers on the liner, he was hoping, if not for a storm, at least for some weather rough enough to slow the ship down.

It all had to do with the important matter of the ship's sweep.

Each day on the homeward journey the man in charge of the entertainments on board had run a 'sweep' in which passengers had been invited to say in advance how many miles the ship would travel during the following twenty-four hours. The entrance fee was sixpence and the prize money went to the person who came nearest to guessing the right answer.

Paddington had had several pretend goes during the

voyage, but that morning he had for the very first time, and after a great deal of thought, actually invested his last remaining sixpence on a ticket.

In the hope that something unexpected might happen to slow the *Karenia* down before it reached port he'd made a wild guess lower than anyone else's. However, now that he'd had time to view the weather he was beginning to regret his haste, for as far as the eye could see there wasn't a cloud in the sky. The sea was as calm as the proverbial mill pond and if anything the ship seemed to be going faster than ever before.

Paddington turned away from the rail, gave a deep sigh, and made his way along the deck towards the group of Browns.

He was a hopeful bear at heart and despite the calm

weather he still nursed a faint hope that something would happen which would cause the ship to slow down before the next morning. Losing sixpence was bad enough at the best of times, but when it was your last one matters became ten times worse, and he was just toying with the idea of approaching the man in charge of the entertainments to see if he could get his money back when Mr Brown broke into his thoughts with the news of the party that evening.

Paddington liked parties, especially unexpected ones, and when he heard that the one that evening was to be a fancy dress one with everyone in costume he quickly forgot about the problem of the sweep in the excitement of the moment.

'I don't think I've ever been to a party on a ship before, Mr Brown,' he exclaimed.

'Neither have I, come to that,' admitted Mr Brown. 'I must say I'm looking forward to it.'

'They've got Barry Baird as Master of Ceremonies,' said Jonathan. 'He's the chap we've seen on television.'

'He takes things out of people's pockets without them knowing,' said Judy.

'And he hypnotises people as well,' added Jonathan.

Mr Brown rose to his feet. 'I can see we'd better go along to the entertainments office and make sure of getting some costumes,' he said. 'Otherwise there'll be some long faces to-night if they're all gone.'

'Bags I go as Robin Hood!' exclaimed Jonathan.

'I rather fancy myself as Mark Anthony,' said Mr

Brown thoughtfully. 'How about you, Paddington?'

But Paddington had already disappeared along the deck. It wasn't often he was allowed to dress up, and when it was dressing up and a ship's party and an entertainment all rolled into one, then he was anxious to make sure of matters by being first in the queue.

Paddington wasn't the only one looking forward to the coming party. Gradually, as the day wore on, bunting and other decorations began to appear over the ship and as the time for the party drew near strangely clad figures were to be seen flitting around the decks with an air of half-suppressed excitement.

'I reckon Paddington could go as himself,' said Mr Brown, as they stood waiting for him by the entrance to the dance floor. 'I've seen at least six bears already.'

'Mercy me!' exclaimed Mrs Bird. 'This isn't him coming now, is it?' She pointed with her umbrella towards an approaching figure clad in what seemed to be a costume made up of several lengths of black concertina and a piece of white cardboard.

'It's Paddington all right,' said Judy. 'That's his hat.'

'I don't think it really goes with evening dress,' said Mrs Brown. 'It makes him look rather like a penguin after a night out.'

'A penguin!' exclaimed Paddington, looking most upset as he caught Mrs Brown's words. 'I'm Beau Brummel – the famous dandy.'

'Beau Brummel!' echoed Jonathan. 'I thought he died a long time before evening dress.'

'I must say you look more like a bow window to me,' said Mr Brown, as he examined Paddington's shirt front.

Paddington began to look more and more upset as he listened to the others. 'They didn't have many costumes my size left,' he explained, giving Mr Brown a hard stare.

'Well, I'm sure he didn't have marmalade stains down his front, whoever he was,' said Mr Brown lamely, as his wife dug him in the ribs.

'That's not marmalade, Mr Brown,' exclaimed Paddington. 'That's glue!'

'Glue!' repeated Mr Brown. 'How on earth did you manage to get glue down your front?'

'I'm afraid I had a bit of trouble with my dicky,' explained Paddington. 'It's a bit difficult with paws and it kept rolling up, so I had to borrow some special glue from the carpenter's shop.'

The Browns exchanged glances. 'Well, they did say come as you like,' said Mr Brown.

'Quite right,' said Mrs Bird, as she followed Mr Brown into the ballroom. 'And as no one here has ever met Beau Brummel, who are they to judge?'

'I think you look jolly smart anyway, Paddington,' said Judy, squeezing his paw as they made their way across the floor in the direction of the band.

Paddington was very keen on bands, especially when they played loudly, and the ship's band, although it was only small, seemed unusually good value in this respect, particularly as several of the musicians had to play more than one instrument.

At the end of the first number he joined in the applause and then settled back in his seat as the leader, having bowed several times to the audience, raised his hand and signalled a fanfare on the trumpets to herald the arrival on stage of Bouncing Barry Baird, the Master of Ceremonies.

'Are you all right, Paddington?' asked Mrs Brown, as she saw him examining his paws with interest.

'I think so, thank you, Mrs Brown,' replied Paddington vaguely. 'But I think something's gone wrong with my claps.'

Mrs Brown opened her mouth but then, as the applause died down, decided against it. There were some things better not inquired in to, especially when they were to do with Paddington.

Up on the small stage Bouncing Barry Baird clasped the microphone as if it was a stick of rock and beamed at the audience. 'Hallo! Hallo! Hallo!' he boomed. 'How are all me old shipmates?'

'All right, thank you, Mr Baird,' exclaimed Paddington from his position in the front row, raising his hat politely.

Barry Baird seemed slightly taken aback at receiving a reply to his question. 'I've got the bird before now,' he said, looking at Paddington's costume, 'but never quite so early in the act.'

'I can see you've got your furbelows on, bear,' he continued, pointing towards Paddington. 'In fact, come to think of it, you've even got fur below your furbelows!'

In the applause which followed, Paddington gave Barry Baird a particularly hard stare. Catching sight of it suddenly Mr Baird hastily averted his eyes and went on with his act.

'What is it?' he asked. 'What is it – and I'm offering no prizes for the answer – what is it that has a green head, six furry legs and one purple eye?'

'I don't know either, Mr Baird,' called out Paddington, who had seen Barry Baird's act several times before on television, 'but there's one on your back!'

The applause which followed Paddington's remark was even greater than it had been for Barry Baird and as it echoed round the ballroom the comedian put his hand over the microphone, leant over the footlights, and glared down at Paddington. 'Barry Baird does the funnies here, bear,' he hissed.

'So much for wit and humour,' he announced, as he straightened up and showed a row of gleaming white teeth to the audience. 'Now we come to the serious part of the show. The fastest act you've ever seen, ladies and gentlemen. Before your very eyes – no mirrors – no deception – before your very eyes I will remove the entire contents of the pockets belonging to any gentleman in the audience who cares to step up here – and he'll never know it happened! Now come along, ladies and gentlemen, all I'm asking for is one volunteer . . .'

'Oh, crikey!' groaned Jonathan, as there was a sudden movement from the front row. 'Trust Paddington!'

Barry Baird seemed to lose some of his bounce as Paddington climbed up on to the stage, but he quickly recovered himself.

'A big hand, ladies and gentlemen,' he boomed. 'A big hand for this young bear gentleman who's volunteered to have his pockets picked.'

'He'll be lucky if he gets anything out of Paddington's pockets,' murmured Mr Brown.

Barry Baird signalled to the band to start playing and then, talking all the while, he hovered round Paddington, his hands gliding up and down through the air like two serpents.

There was a gasp of amazement from the audience as he held up first a pencil then a notebook for them to see. Paddington himself looked as surprised as anyone for he hadn't felt a thing.

Signalling to the band to play even faster, Barry Baird, his white teeth gleaming in the spotlight, circled the stage once more, waving his arms in time to the music.

Suddenly he stopped and the expression froze on his face as he slowly withdrew his hand from one of Paddington's side pockets.

'Uggh!' he exclaimed before he could stop himself. 'What have you got in there, bear?'

Paddington examined Barry Baird's hand with interest as the music came to a stop. 'I expect that's a marmalade sandwich, Mr Baird,' he replied cheerfully. 'I put it in there in case I had an emergency. I'm afraid it's a bit squashed.'

Barry Baird, who looked as if he was about to have a bit of an emergency himself, stared at his hand for a moment as if he could hardly believe his eyes, and then gave a rather high pitched laugh as he turned to face the audience.

'I've been in some jams before now,' he announced feebly, 'but this is the first time I've ever been in a marmalade sandwich!'

Wiping his hands on a small square of silk which he withdrew from his top pocket Barry Baird mopped his brow and held up his hand for silence as he turned hurriedly to the next part of his act.

'I want everyone,' he announced, 'to raise their hands above their heads and clasp them together.'

While the audience did as they were told Barry Baird took a length of string from his pocket, tied a key to one end, and then set it in motion like a pendulum.

'Now,' he said as the main lights went dim again and the swinging key was illuminated by a single spotlight. 'I want you all to watch this key carefully as it goes from left . . . to right . . . to left . . . to right . . . to left . . .' Barry Baird's voice grew soft and caressing as the light went lower.

'I've seen this trick done before,' whispered Mr Brown with a chuckle. 'You wait till they put the lights up again. There's always some chap who can't get his hands apart again.'

'Gosh!' groaned Judy, as the lights suddenly went up and everyone relaxed. 'Look who it is!'

'I *am* surprised,' said Mrs Bird. 'I should have thought Paddington would be more likely to hypnotise Barry Baird than be put under himself. Some of those stares he's been giving him have been very hard.'

The audience fell silent as they watched Paddington struggle to try and unlock his paws and even Barry Baird himself seemed slightly taken aback at the success of his trick.

'Never mind, bear,' he exclaimed. 'I'll soon have them apart.'

Without further ado he stood in front of Paddington and made several violent passes, clicking his fingers as he did so.

The audience grew even quieter as Paddington's struggles grew more violent and Barry Baird's efforts to free him were obviously in vain.

After some minutes Barry Baird ushered Paddington behind some curtains and then came back on to the stage.

'I'm sorry,' he announced, looking rather red in the face. 'That young bear's still under the influence. We

shall just have to hope it wears off in time.'

Barry Baird made a half-hearted attempt to carry on with his act but somehow the spell had gone for most of his audience and certainly for the Browns as they hurried out of the hall and round to the back in order to find Paddington.

'Where on earth can he have got to?' exclaimed

Mr Brown after they had searched the immediate vicinity without success.

'He can't have gone far,' said Mrs Brown. 'Not with his paws over his head like that.'

'Perhaps he's gone back to his cabin,' said one of the stewards who'd been helping in the search. He led the way along a corridor and opened a door at the end.

'No,' he said. 'Not a sausage – let alone a bear.'

'Never mind,' said Mr Brown. 'We'll wait in here for a few minutes. He's bound to turn up sooner or later.'

Mr Brown tried to sound cheerful but as they settled down to wait and the minutes ticked by even he began to find it more and more difficult.

'You don't think . . .' began Mrs Brown anxiously after some time had passed. 'I mean . . . he couldn't have fallen overboard or anything, could he?'

'If he has and he's still got his paws fixed together . . .' began Judy.

'Knowing Paddington,' said Mr Brown hastily, 'he's much more likely to have fallen in a bowl of dough at the bakery.' He rose and looked at his watch again. 'All the same,' he continued, 'I think it's about time we did something about it. Though where we're going to start goodness only knows.'

Mrs Bird gripped her umbrella. 'I know where *I'm* going to start,' she said firmly. 'With the Captain.'

With that she stalked off down the corridor leaving

the rest of the family looking, if possible, even more worried than before.

Although Mrs Bird was very firm with Paddington at times, she was no respecter of persons when it came to looking after his interests and it was obvious a little later on by the sudden surge of activity on board the ship that she had got her way with the powers that be.

Men started running urgently about the decks, somewhere far below an alarm bell began to ring, and shortly after that with a series of blasts on its siren the great ship started to lose speed.

'Crikey!' exclaimed Jonathan, as a loud clanking noise came from the bows of the ship. 'Things must be serious. They're getting ready to drop anchor!'

The Captain of the *Karenia* looked up from his desk at the gathering before him.

It was the following morning and not only the Browns but quite a number of the ship's crew had been called to his cabin in order to investigate the events of the evening before.

'So, this is the young bear who caused all the trouble, is it?' he asked, staring at Paddington.

'I don't think it was his fault,' explained the Chief Engineer, coming to his rescue. 'If only someone had shouted "bear overboard" instead of "man overboard," I'd have known. I had him down in my workshop all the time trying to get his paws apart.'

'What I don't understand, Paddington,' said Mr Brown, 'is why you couldn't get them apart in the first place.'

'It was that special glue I used for my dicky, Mr Brown,' explained Paddington. 'I must have left some on my paws by mistake.'

'Then when he put them together he couldn't pull them apart again,' said Barry Baird, looking much more cheerful than he had done the previous evening. 'Must admit it had me worried at the time.'

'It's like that glue I've got in my carpentry set, Dad,' said Jonathan. 'It's some new stuff and it only works if you get it on both surfaces.'

'I must have got it on both my surfaces,' added Paddington. 'That's why my claps went funny.'

'And by golly,' said the Chief Engineer, 'when it does stick – it sticks. Quite a job that young bear gave me.'

'I suppose you realise,' said the Captain, 'you caused me to heave to last night?'

'Heave *two*?' exclaimed Paddington with interest.

'Not *two*, Paddington,' explained Judy. 'To. That's quite a different matter. The Captain means he had to stop the ship because he thought you'd fallen overboard.'

'Been on this run since I was a boy,' said the Captain gruffly. 'Never had a man overboard yet, let alone a bear.'

'You didn't really have one this time, did you?' said

Judy bravely.

The Captain thought for a moment. 'True enough, young lady,' he said at last. 'Only trouble is I've got to write me log out and it doesn't look very good. Takes a bit of explainin'. Especially when the same bear wins the ship's sweep because we didn't make as many miles yesterday as everyone else thought we would!'

'What!' echoed Paddington, hardly able to believe his ears. 'I've won the ship's sweep?'

'Ten pounds, fifteen shillings and sixpence,' broke in the first officer, handing over a large envelope. 'I should count it to make sure it's all there.'

'Congratulations, bear,' said the Captain, taking hold of Paddington's other paw. 'Mind you,' he added sternly, 'if you travel in my ship again you'd better not let it happen twice. Otherwise me suspicions might get aroused and I'll have to clap you in irons.'

Paddington looked most alarmed at the Captain's words. 'I don't think I shall be going to Peru again for quite a long time,' he announced hastily.

The Captain broke into a broad smile. 'In that case,' he said, looking at the clock, 'seeing we're nearly back in England I suggest we all adjourn to my table for breakfast. Might not get the chance again.'

'Well, I think you're very lucky, Paddington,' said Mrs Brown, as they followed the others down a long corridor. 'It's not many bears who have the honour of being invited to sit at the Captain's table.'

The Captain paused as they entered the dining-room. 'Come to think of it,' he said, 'I don't know as I've had the honour of askin' one before. Especially one who's just won one of me sweeps.'

3.
Paddington
Buys a Share

On the first day of his return to number thirty-two Windsor Gardens Paddington was extremely busy. Apart from all the unpacking he had to do there were visits to be paid, stories to be told – not once, but time and time again – cupboards to be investigated, old and familiar chairs to be sat in; in fact, all the thousand and one things to do with settling down once more into a normal life at his old home.

Everyone was so pleased to see him and to hear all about his trip that the hours seemed to melt away and by the time he went to bed that evening he felt as if he hadn't been away at all.

After weeks of sleeping in a bunk it was nice to be back in his old bed, especially as during his absence Mr Brown had redecorated his room so that it now had powder-blue walls and gleaming white, freshly painted woodwork, not to mention a notice board for his day-to-day reminders and a brand-new carpet on the floor.

'The old one was getting rather threadbare,' explained Mrs Brown, when she brought him his breakfast in bed the following morning. 'We've bought you a patterned one so that it won't show your stains quite so much.'

'My *stains*, Mrs Brown,' exclaimed Paddington, looking most offended as he sat up in bed rubbing his eyes.

'Your stains,' repeated Mrs Bird sternly, letting in a flood of sunshine as she drew the curtains. 'The old carpet was so stiff with dried marmalade we practically had to saw it in two to get it out of the room.'

Mrs Brown looked nervously at Paddington. 'Have you anything planned for this morning?' she asked.

Paddington dipped his paw thoughtfully into the jar of marmalade. 'Not really, Mrs Brown,' he announced vaguely. 'There's some special shopping to do and I want to put my winnings in the bank for safety.'

'A very good idea,' said Mrs Brown. 'I don't like to think of you carrying all that money around in your suitcase. You never know what may happen.'

Mrs Brown looked most relieved at Paddington's reply. Things had been unusually quiet just lately at number thirty-two Windsor Gardens and she'd woken that morning with the nasty feeling that the peace of recent weeks was about to be shattered.

'I shouldn't go counting your chickens before

they're hatched,' said Mrs Bird grimly, when Mrs Brown gave voice to her thoughts as they were going back downstairs.

Although she didn't say anything, the Browns' housekeeper also had the feeling that she was witnessing the quiet before the storm. Nevertheless, try as she might, even Mrs Bird could find little to grumble at when Paddington appeared at the kitchen door some while later, dressed and ready to greet the morning air.

His fur was well brushed and even his old duffle coat looked unusually respectable as he disappeared out of the house and hurried off down the road in the direction of the Portobello market, carrying his suitcase in one paw and an important looking booklet marked FFLOYDS BANK in the other.

Pausing only to call in at the baker's in order to renew his standing order for buns and to have a chat about his various experiences while he'd been away, he hurried on towards the antique shop run by his friend, Mr Gruber.

Normally Paddington shared his elevenses with Mr Gruber, and he wanted to warn his friend that he might be a little late that morning.

Paddington was a popular bear with the traders in the market and his progress down the Portobello Road was much slower than he had intended so that, what with one thing and another, by the time he reached the bank it was almost ten o'clock.

However, he was pleased to see that he was first in

the queue and after looking round carefully to make sure no one was watching he settled himself down on the pavement, withdrew the bundle of notes from his suitcase, and began counting them once again in order to make sure they were all there.

Paddington had had an account with the local branch of Ffloyds for some time, but although he occasionally paid them a visit in order to have a chat with the manager and to make sure everything was all right, it wasn't often he had the opportunity to put any actual money in and he was looking forward to the event.

The notes were crisp and new and rather difficult to

separate with paws so that in no time at all he became lost to the outside world and it wasn't until a shadow fell across the pavement that he realised anyone else was about.

Hurriedly stuffing the money under his duffle coat, Paddington looked up to meet the gaze of a tall, rather distinguished looking man in a black overcoat and bowler hat.

The man raised his hat politely. 'Pardon me, bear,' he said. 'I couldn't help noticing what you were doing and I wondered if we were here on the same mission.'

Not to be outdone, Paddington jumped to his feet, still clutching the money tightly beneath a fold in his duffle coat, and raised his own hat with a free paw. 'I don't think I'm here on a mission,' he replied. 'I've come to put my money in the bank.'

'Look after the pennies,' said the man approvingly, 'and the pounds will look after themselves. That's what I always say.'

'Oh, they're not pennies,' said Paddington importantly. 'They're pounds. I won over ten on a ship's sweep.'

'Ten pounds!' echoed the man with interest. 'You don't mean to tell me you're putting it all into the bank?'

'Not all ten pounds,' said Paddington. 'I want to save part of it to buy some presents.'

The man took hold of Paddington's arm and led him a little way along the street. 'What a good thing we met,' he exclaimed. 'It must have been fate.' He looked all round and then lowered his voice confidingly. 'Now, if you'd told me you were taking your money *out*, I'd

have understood. Between you, me and the gatepost, all's not well with Ffloyds.'

Paddington's eyes grew larger as he listened. 'What!' he exclaimed hotly. 'All's not well with Ffloyds!'

'Ssh!' The man put his finger to his lips as he drew Paddington into a nearby doorway. 'Not too loud, bear,' he said hastily. 'You might start a panic and then there's no knowing what'll happen.'

He peered out into the street and then eyed Paddington thoughtfully as if trying to make up his mind whether he could trust him or not. 'You look like a bear of the world,' he said at last. 'I wonder . . . can you tell me what we're standing on at this moment?'

Paddington looked most surprised at the question. 'A paving stone,' he answered promptly.

'Aha!' said the man. 'But can you tell me what's underneath that?'

'Earth,' said Paddington doubtfully.

The man gave a chuckle and then withdrew a small glass phial of dark liquid from an inside pocket. 'I'll let you into a secret, bear,' he said, as he held it up to the light. 'Oil! That's what we're standing on. Millions of pounds' worth of oil.' He pointed towards a dark patch on the road near by. 'Ninety-nine people out of a hundred,' he continued, 'would say that had dripped from a car. They don't realise it's seeping up *through* the ground under their very feet. I tell you . . . anyone who buys a share in the Portobello Oil Company now is going to make a fortune out of the interest alone.'

'The Portobello Oil Company?' exclaimed Paddington. 'I don't think I've ever heard of that before.'

The man felt in his pocket again. 'Not many people have,' he replied. 'It hasn't been going very long.'

'Look here, bear,' he said, as he held out a piece of paper. 'I must say I've taken a liking to you. These shares are really worth fifteen pounds each but I think I could manage to let you have one for ten.'

Paddington looked at the man doubtfully. 'It's very kind of you,' he said. 'But I don't think I could afford *ten* pounds. I really wanted to buy some presents as well.'

'Nonsense!' said the man briskly, as he crossed off the word FIFTEEN on the piece of paper and wrote in the word TEN. 'You'll be able to buy all the presents you need with the interest – and more besides.'

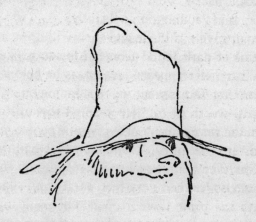

Before Paddington had a chance to even open his mouth let alone say anything he found himself clutching the share while the man quickly transferred the bundle of notes from his paw to an inside pocket.

'Now, don't forget,' he warned. 'Not a word to anyone. I don't want the news to get around. At least, not until the derricks arrive and then you can tell anyone you like.'

'The derricks?' repeated Paddington.

'The oil-drilling equipment,' explained the man. 'I

have to go and see about them this morning.'

'When do I collect my interest?' asked Paddington anxiously.

The man chuckled. 'I can see you have an eye to business,' he said. 'A bear after my own heart. If you care to meet me here to-morrow morning.— same time — same place, I'll see what I can do. But remember,' he whispered. 'Keep it under your hat. We don't want the bottom to drop out of the market.'

With that he gave a final wave of his rolled umbrella and then hurried off up the Portobello Road leaving Paddington standing on the pavement looking at his piece of paper with an excited gleam in his eyes.

It was an impressive-looking document, covered with a flowery sort of print which was rather difficult to read. Studying it he was just able to make out the words PORTOBELLO OIL COMPANY across the top, but underneath the print was so small and there was so much of it he soon decided he would have to take it home and examine it more closely at his leisure.

Remembering the man's instructions, he folded the piece of paper carefully into four and then placed it under his hat for safety.

Paddington had never owned any sort of share before, let alone a ten-pound one in an oil company, and he felt most important as he made his way back along the road. All the same, he trod very carefully when he crossed over to the other side in the direction of the shops. Apart from telling him to keep the matter under

his hat the man had also said something about not
wanting the bottom to drop out of the market and he
wasn't the sort of bear to take any unnecessary
chances.

When he reached the other side of the road Paddington hesitated for a moment outside the window of a
small store. There was a thoughtful expression on his
face as he peered through the glass at the various items
on display.

Although he'd brought home several small presents
for the Browns he was anxious to buy them something
really nice in return for their kindness in paying for
his trip to Peru.

With the interest on his new share Paddington felt

sure he would be able to buy some very good presents indeed and he felt equally certain that the owner of the shop would be only too pleased to wait until the next day for his money, for despite his habit of driving a hard bargain, all the shopkeepers and other dealers in the market held Paddington in high regard.

With the promise of riches to come Paddington took rather longer over his shopping that morning than he'd at first intended and by the time he reached Mr Gruber's antique shop for elevenses his friend was already waiting anxiously outside.

'I began to think you weren't coming, Mr Brown!' he exclaimed. 'I had to put a saucer over your mug so that the cocoa wouldn't get cold.'

Paddington sank gratefully into one of the deck-chairs on the pavement while Mr Gruber bustled around setting a tray of buns on a nearby table. 'I've been buying a few coming-home presents, Mr Gruber,' he explained.

Mr Gruber looked at him reprovingly over the top of his glasses. 'It's very thoughtful of you, Mr Brown,' he said, 'and I'm sure everyone will be most grateful, but I hope you've left yourself some money to put in the bank for a rainy day.

'There have been one or two rather nasty cases of fraud in the market just lately,' he continued, before Paddington could reply. 'I was very pleased this morning when you told me you were putting your money in a safe place.'

Mr Gruber settled himself in a deck-chair alongside Paddington and sipped his cocoa. 'It seems that someone has been going around selling false shares for a firm called the Portobello Oil Company. You'll find this difficult to believe, Mr Brown, but one or two foolish people have actually bought one!'

Mr Gruber looked at Paddington with some concern as a loud choking sound came from behind his cocoa mug. 'I do hope it's not too hot, Mr Brown,' he exclaimed.

'It's all right, Mr Gruber,' gasped Paddington hastily. 'I was having trouble with one of my buns. I think a currant must have gone down the wrong way.'

Mr Gruber gave Paddington a pat on the back and then settled himself once again in order to resume his story.

'The man they're after,' he said, 'is called "Jim the Dandy".'

' "Jim the Dandy"?' echoed Paddington, looking more and more worried.

'That's right,' said Mr Gruber. 'They call him that because of the way he dresses. Just like someone who works in the City. In fact, you'd have a job to tell him from the real thing.'

'I hope they catch him soon,' he continued, 'otherwise he'll begin to give the market a bad name. I was talking to a policeman only yesterday and he agreed with me that there's only one thing worse than selling something that isn't there to sell, and that's buying something and not paying for it.'

Mr Gruber shook his head sadly. 'There's been quite a bit of that going on just lately, too, Mr Brown,' he added. 'But I'm pleased to say the police are hot on the trail of the culprits. I only hope when they do catch up with them they'll get what they deserve.'

Mr Gruber broke off as before his astonished gaze Paddington suddenly jumped out of his chair, removed his overcoat and hastily bundled it over his pile of shopping. 'Are you sure you're feeling all right, Mr Brown?' he asked anxiously. 'I must say you don't look too good.'

Paddington gave a worried glance up and down the market. '*I'm* all right, thank you very much, Mr Gruber,' he said mysteriously. 'But I'm not too sure about things in general!'

Mr Gruber knew better than to inquire into matters which might be difficult to explain. All the same, he began to look more and more concerned as Paddington slumped back into his chair leaving a half-eaten bun untouched on the plate by his side.

But if Mr Gruber looked worried, Paddington himself was even more woebegone. His face had been long enough to start with, but it lengthened still further some while later as he made his way back towards Windsor Gardens and had time to consider all that had happened that morning.

By the time he reached the familiar green front door of number thirty-two his face had fallen to its longest ever, but by then his hat was pulled down so well over his forehead, and his head had sunk so low into his shoulders that only the closest observer would have noticed anything amiss.

Paddington lifted the brim of his hat, gave one last worried glance up and down Windsor Gardens, and then disappeared from view, closing the door behind him with a loud click which seemed to suggest that one member of the Brown family at least wouldn't be receiving any more visitors that day.

4.
A Visit to the Stock Exchange

Mrs Bird was the first member of the household to notice the change that had suddenly come over Paddington.

'I can't understand it,' she remarked the following day. 'He was so bright and cheerful yesterday morning. Now he looks as if he's got all the cares in the world on his shoulders.'

'I do hope it's not the after-effects of all his travelling,' said Mrs Brown.

'Whatever it is it happened when he went out shopping in the market,' said Mrs Bird decidedly. 'He came back afterwards looking very down in the mouth and he didn't even finish his treacle pudding at lunch time.'

'I must admit he has been acting rather strangely,' agreed Mrs Brown. 'I caught him drilling a hole in the garden with Henry's brace and bit yesterday afternoon. He seemed most upset about something.'

'If you ask me,' said Mrs Bird decidedly, 'it's got something to do with money.'

'Money?' Mrs Brown began to look even more worried. 'Whatever makes you say that?'

'He spent all yesterday evening doing his accounts,' said Mrs Bird darkly. 'And when he'd finished he wanted to borrow the red ink!'

'Besides,' she continued, 'there was that business with the paper this morning, *and* he was asking Mr Brown a lot of very odd questions at breakfast.'

Mr Brown worked in the City of London and every breakfast-time before going to his office he studied a special newspaper which was all about stocks and shares. That very morning he'd discovered that one of the middle pages was missing. No one had owned up to taking it but at the time Mrs Bird had had her suspicions as to the culprit, and now she was certain.

'That young bear's up to something,' she exclaimed. 'He had a bath of his own accord last night – that's always a bad sign. And when he went out this morning he was all dressed up. I don't like the look of things at all.'

Mrs Bird attacked the corner of the dining-room with a feather duster in order to emphasise her words as she looked out of the window. But keen though her eyesight was it would have had to penetrate not only a good many buildings but quite a few other objects on the way as well to have caught even a glimpse of Paddington.

For, apart from being a good many miles away, the object of her suspicions was also at that moment effectively hidden behind a seething mass of dark suits, bowler hats, brief-cases, and rolled umbrellas.

In fact, as he emerged from the depths of the underground and found himself being carried along the pavement like a cork in a millstream, Paddington decided he couldn't remember ever having been in such a crowd before.

Fortunately the tide soon divided itself into a number of smaller streams and after a good deal of struggling he eventually managed to force his way in the direction he wanted to go until at long last he found himself in a much narrower street at the end of which stood a tall, important-looking building.

After carefully consulting his map in order to make sure he was in the right place, Paddington took a deep breath and pushed open the door.

He stood for a moment with wide-open eyes as he took in the scene all around him. Everywhere men were rushing hither and thither carrying brief-cases or pieces of paper as they went about their business. If the pavement outside had been crowded the inside of the building by comparison seemed like a gigantic ant heap, and Paddington was about to explore farther

when a heavy hand descended on to his shoulder and
held him in a vice-like grip. ' 'ere,' said a gruff voice.
'What are you a-doing of?'

Paddington jumped and turned to see a man in a
dark blue uniform and a silk hat staring down at him.

'I suppose you know this is the Stock Exchange?' said the man sternly.

'Oh, yes,' replied Paddington importantly. 'That's why I'm here. I've come to exchange one of my stocks.'

'You've *what*?' The man looked at Paddington suspiciously. 'Are you trying to pull my leg, bear?'

'Oh, no,' said Paddington earnestly, as he undid his suitcase and withdrew his share. 'I've come all the way from Windsor Gardens especially to do it.'

'Oh, dear,' said the man, his expression softening slightly. 'I'm afraid I can't help you then.'

'Mind you,' he added, as he caught sight of the disappointed look on Paddington's face, 'if there's anything else I can do I'll be only too pleased. Us waiters is here to oblige.'

At the sound of the man's words Paddington brightened considerably. It had been a long journey all the way from Windsor Gardens in the crowded tube train and he was feeling hot and thirsty. Mr Brown had answered a lot of his questions about the Stock Exchange but he certainly hadn't mentioned anything about there being free refreshments and it seemed a very good idea indeed.

'I think I'd like a bun and a cup of cocoa, please,' he announced.

To his surprise the helpful expression on the man's face disappeared as if by magic and was replaced almost immediately by one he didn't like the look of at all.

'A *bun*!' exclaimed the man. 'And a cup of *cocoa*! I'll have you know this is a place of business, not a café. Just because I'm called a waiter it doesn't mean to say I've got nothing better to do than serve young bears with cocoa of a morning.'

Paddington's face dropped as he listened to the man explain that Stock Exchange waiters were quite different to any other kind and really had nothing at all to do with food and drink.

'Anyway,' concluded the man, 'I'm afraid you can't come in and that's that. The Stock Exchange is for members only. It's like a club, you know – and a very h'exclusive one at that,' he added haughtily.

'Perhaps I could join,' said Paddington hopefully, as he felt in his duffle coat pocket for a sixpence.

'Join?' The waiter gave a hollow laugh. 'You can't join just like that you know. Why, bless me, there's all sorts of things you have to do first. You'd have to 'ave your *bona fides* checked for a start.'

'Have my *bona fides* checked!' exclaimed Paddington, looking most upset. 'I don't think I've got any.'

'Well you certainly can't come in in that case,' said the waiter. '*Bona fides*,' he continued in a superior tone of voice, 'is something you either 'as or you 'asn't. They 'as to do with your forebears.'

'My *four* bears?' repeated Paddington, looking even more puzzled. 'I've only got one bear. There's my Aunt Lucy in Peru. That's where I come from – Darkest Peru. But I don't think I've got four.'

The waiter began to breathe rather heavily. He'd had some difficult customers to deal with during the years he'd spent on the Stock Exchange, but this was one of the worst he could remember.

'That's enough of that,' he said sternly. 'I think you'd best be cutting along now. I've got work to do and it doesn't h'include chatting with young bears trying to get theirselves free snacks of a morning.'

Looking most upset at the way things were turning

out, Paddington began unlocking his suitcase. 'I only wanted to change my stocks,' he exclaimed. 'It's for the Portobello Oil Company and I don't think it's any good because . . .'

'What's that?' exclaimed the man. 'Did I hear you say you've got a share what's no good?' He reached down and examined the piece of paper in Paddington's paw. 'Where did you get this, bear?' he continued, as he guided Paddington across the floor in the direction of a door to one side of the hall.

'I bought it in the Portobello Market,' explained Paddington, pleased that he was getting somewhere at last. 'Only I don't think it's a very good one because the man didn't turn up with my interest. So I thought I'd try and change it for another one instead.'

'Just wait here, bear,' continued the man casually, as he ushered Paddington into a room full of deep leather arm-chairs. 'I shan't keep you a moment.'

As the door clicked shut behind the waiter, Paddington looked all around the room, picked on the deepest and most comfortable-looking arm-chair, and settled himself inside it with a pleased expression on his face. From past experience he'd always found that if you went to the right people and kept on long enough things had a habit of turning out right in the end.

All the same, as the minutes ticked by and no one came to see him, Paddington began to look slightly more worried and he was relieved when at long last footsteps approached from the outside and the door was flung open to reveal the waiter. To his surprise two other men in raincoats and trilby hats were standing there as well.

'That's 'im,' said the waiter, pointing at Paddington.

The first of the two men entered the room and waved a card. 'Police,' he said briefly. 'I'm afraid we must take you along to the station . . .'

'Take me to the station!' repeated Paddington, looking most surprised. 'But I've only just got here.'

The man gave him a nasty look. 'Take you along to the *police* station,' he repeated heavily. 'Where you will be remanded in custody while we make further inquiries.'

Paddington jumped to his feet in alarm. 'Remanded in *custard*!' he exclaimed. 'I don't think Mrs Bird will like that very much. It'll make my fur all matted.'

The two men in plain clothes exchanged glances. 'Clever disguise,' said the second one, ignoring Paddington's interruption. 'I always pictured "Jim the Dandy" as being much taller somehow.'

' "Jim the Dandy"!' echoed Paddington.

'Would have had me fooled,' agreed the first man, turning an equally deaf ear. 'And I've been through the Rogues' Gallery twice. Only shows you can't always go by people's descriptions.'

'Will there be a reward?' asked the waiter hopefully.

'Shouldn't be surprised,' replied the first man. 'We've been on the lookout for this character for some time. One of the cleverest confidence tricksters seen in London for many a year. Dud shares – forgery – false passports – there's a list as long as your arm.'

'He'll be in prison for a good long stretch, you mark my words,' agreed the second man.

Paddington looked from one to the other of the three men. 'In prison!' he exclaimed in alarm. 'But I only wanted to exchange my stocks!'

'Ha! Tell that to the judge,' replied the first man. 'Selling dud shares is a serious offence.'

'But I didn't sell it,' cried Paddington, waving his piece of paper wildly in the air. 'I bought it. It cost me ten pounds. All the notes had my special paw mark on *and* I wrote the numbers down on this share!'

'What's that?' One of the detectives took the piece of paper from Paddington's paw and examined it with interest. 'You wrote all the numbers down?' His voice broke off as Paddington suddenly shot past like a bullet out of a gun. 'Hey! Stop!' he yelled.

'Come back!' cried the other man.

But before either of them had time to move Paddington had disappeared through the door. He cast some anxious glances over his shoulder, took a hurried look at the main door where another waiter, attracted by the noise, stood barring his way, and then turned and headed towards the main body of the building.

For the first time that morning Paddington felt pleased that the Stock Exchange was such a crowded place of business. He still wasn't sure what all the fuss was about but from where he'd been standing he hadn't liked the look of things at all. There were times when disappearing was much better than staying and trying to explain matters, and for someone who wanted to disappear in a hurry the Stock Exchange would have been hard to beat.

Mrs Brown stood at the front door of number thirty-two Windsor Gardens and looked anxiously at the two men on her step.

'Paddington?' she repeated. 'Did you say you want to see Paddington?'

'That's right, ma'am,' replied one of the men. He consulted a piece of paper in his hand. 'This share's got his name and address on it. *And* some kind of paw mark.'

'I expect that's to show it's genuine,' said Mrs Brown doubtfully. 'He usually does that. But it's rather early. Couldn't you come back later?'

'We're from Scotland Yard,' broke in the second man, waving a card in the air. 'We're rather anxious to see him about a certain matter that occurred yesterday.'

'Scotland Yard!' Mrs Brown clutched at the door frame for support, but before she had time to go any deeper into the matter Mrs Bird came bustling up the hall.

'What on earth's going on?' she asked crossly. 'I'm waiting to serve the breakfast. It's bad enough not being able to find Paddington without . . .' Her voice broke off as she caught sight of the look on Mrs Brown's face. 'There's nothing wrong, is there?' she asked anxiously.

'Bless you no, ma'am,' replied the second detective. 'We only want to give him his notes back.'

'Give him his notes back?' echoed Mrs Brown.

'Then pounds,' said the first detective. 'Thanks to him putting the numbers down we've recovered them all.'

'*And* we've caught the criminal,' said the second man.

'Wish there were more bears about like him,' added the first one. 'There'll be a reward of course, but we'd like to congratulate him personally if we may.'

Mrs Brown and Mrs Bird exchanged glances. 'You'd better come in,' said Mrs Brown weakly.

Neither of them had the slightest idea what the two detectives were talking about, but as Mrs Bird led the way down the hall she nodded towards a door under the stairs.

'You may find him in the coat cupboard,' she said. 'Thinking back I heard some bangs going on in there soon after you rang the bell.'

'Blimey!' said one of the detectives as he bent down to open the door. 'He's worse than the Scarlet Pimpernel.'

'What!' exclaimed Paddington, looking most offended as he emerged from his hiding place under

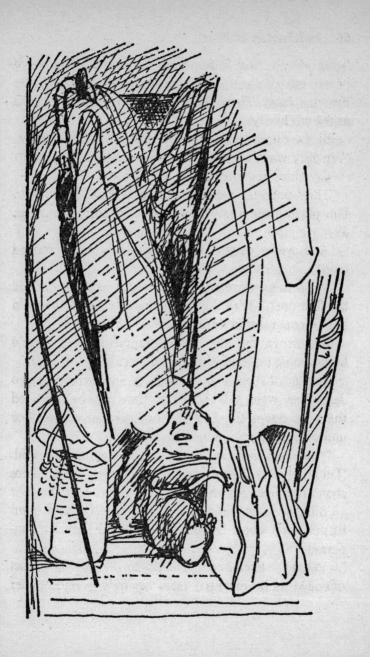

the stairs. 'I'm worse than a scarlet pimple!'

Mrs Bird paused at the kitchen door and gave a sigh. Judging from the look on Paddington's face there were some complicated explanations to come. 'I'll put some more bacon and eggs on,' she said. 'Trailing bears must be hungry work and I have a feeling this may all take rather a long time.'

'Gosh!' said Jonathan later that morning when things were back to normal. 'Fancy Paddington having breakfast with two real detectives. Trust him! I can't wait to tell the chaps at school.'

Mr Brown picked up his newspaper. 'And I can't wait to tell them at the office,' he said, dabbing at his moustache with a serviette. 'I'm about an hour late already.'

'You can't go yet,' said Judy, as she entered the room. 'You've all got to come and see your presents.'

'Our presents!' exclaimed Mr Brown, as he followed Judy into the lounge. 'Don't tell me we've got some more. We've had one lot already.'

'These are special "thank you" ones, Mr Brown,' explained Paddington, as he watched the others unwrap their parcels. 'I can pay for them now I've got my money back.'

'I've got a lovely set of oil paints,' said Judy.

'And I've got a super pair of skates,' added Jonathan, echoing her thanks.

Mrs Brown held up a large square of embroidered

linen. 'What a lovely table-cloth!' she exclaimed. 'How very nice.'

'A pipe,' said Mr Brown opening a small cardboard box. 'Just what I wanted. Couldn't have chosen better myself.'

Mrs Bird's eyes looked suspiciously moist as she held up a pink bed jacket for the others to see. 'My favourite colour,' she said. 'How very kind of you to get things we all need, Paddington. You must have given it a lot of thought.'

'I don't suppose you'll have much money left over after you've paid for all this,' said Mr Brown, when all the excitement had died down, 'but if you care to let me have it I might be able to get hold of one or two real shares for you.'

Paddington thought for a moment. It wasn't that he didn't trust Mr Brown, but all in all he felt he'd had quite enough of stocks and shares for a while. 'I think perhaps I really will put the rest of it in the bank this time,' he announced at last.

'Very wise,' said Mrs Bird approvingly. The Browns' housekeeper was a great believer in banks, especially where bears were concerned.

'Crikey, Dad – look!' exclaimed Jonathan suddenly. He pointed to a headline on the front page of Mr Brown's newspaper. 'BEARS HAVE A HEAVY DAY ON THE STOCK EXCHANGE! It looks as if there might be something in there about Paddington.'

Mr Brown cleared his throat and then paused. He

was about to launch forth into an explanation of the difference between Stock Exchange bears and ordinary ones, and that Stock Exchange bears were really only people who sold shares hoping their value would fall, when he caught his wife's eye.

'After all,' said Mrs Brown, 'what's in a name? Besides, it'll look very nice as a heading for one of the chapters in Paddington's scrap-book.'

'Most impressive,' said Mrs Bird, 'and very apt.'

'In fact,' she added, amid general agreement, 'I don't think even Paddington could have thought of a better heading if he'd written it himself.'

5.
Paddington in a Hole

Mrs Brown turned away from the hall mirror and made a face as the sound of hammering rent the morning air.

'I suppose I mustn't grumble,' she said. 'Henry's been making enough noise himself these past few weeks. But I do wish Mr Curry would hurry up and finish all his jobs. He does go on rather.'

Mrs Bird jabbed at the surrounding air with a large hat pin. 'I wouldn't mind,' she said, 'if they were his own ideas in the first place, but he must always go copying other people. He's even talking now of putting a serving hatch in his kitchen wall!'

Mrs Bird gave one of her 'Mr Curry snorts' as she put some finishing touches to her bonnet. The Browns' neighbour, apart from having a reputation in the district for his meanness, also had a habit of copying other people, and living next door to him the Browns suffered more than most.

During Paddington's absence in Peru, Mr Brown had carried out quite a number of jobs in and around their house. Apart from decorating several of the rooms, he'd also laid a concrete path in the back garden and installed a serving hatch between their kitchen and the dining-room.

Mr Curry had been hard put to it to keep up with all the activity in number thirty-two Windsor Gardens, but only the day before he'd announced in a loud voice his intention of carrying out the last two tasks himself in the near future, and that very morning he'd arrived in his back garden dressed in an old boiler suit in order to make preparations for the path.

'I must say,' began Mrs Brown, 'there are times when I find taking the family all the way across London just to visit the dentist a bit of a nuisance, but I shan't be at all sorry to-day.' She gave a sigh as another burst of hammering echoed between the two buildings. 'Are you sure you don't want to come with us, Paddington?' she called.

Paddington hurried into the hall at the sound of his name. 'No thank you, Mrs Brown,' he exclaimed, when she repeated her question. Although he'd never actually been to a dentist he didn't like the sound of them at all, especially after listening to some of Jonathan's graphic descriptions of what went on.

'I think perhaps I'll stay at home and sit in the garden instead,' he announced before anyone could try and change his mind for him.

Mrs Brown eyed the retreating figure of Paddington as he disappeared into the dining-room. 'You know, it's an extraordinary thing,' she remarked, 'but I do believe he's turned over a new leaf. Do you realise we haven't had a single disaster since he came back from Peru? Not one!'

Mrs Bird hastily touched wood as she made for the front door. 'Don't tempt fate,' she warned. 'That young bear doesn't need any encouragement.'

Mrs Bird wasn't at all happy about leaving Paddington alone in the house so soon after his return. She had decided views about his various activities and the fact that, apart from the business of the share, nothing untoward had happened since his return left her unmoved.

But even the Browns' housekeeper would have been hard put to find fault with Paddington's behaviour, at least for the next few minutes or so, had she been there to see it.

Having finished breakfast he carefully wiped his whiskers on the serviette provided by a hopeful Mrs Brown and then made his way through the french windows and out on to the terrace where he stood for a moment sniffing the morning air.

Paddington liked the summer, especially in Mr Brown's garden, which for a London garden was unusually large and full of flowers and shrubs, each with its own special smell.

But the peace of Paddington's morning was short-

lived, for just as he was making some last-minute adjustments to a deck-chair so that he could sit down for
a while and enjoy the morning sunshine, a familiar
voice rang out over the fence.

'Good morning, bear,' said the voice.

Paddington jumped up. 'Good morning, Mr Curry,'
he said doubtfully, raising his hat politely.

Although he'd several times exchanged waves with
the Browns' next-door neighbour since his return, it
was the first occasion when they'd met face to face
and he was feeling a bit nervous. The last time they'd
actually spoken to each other had been at his going-
away party when he'd not only torn one of Mr Curry's
ten-shilling notes in half but he'd also ripped the lining
of his coat by mistake. Mr Curry had taken it rather
badly at the time and he wasn't at all sure if they were
still on speaking terms.

But for once the Browns' neighbour seemed to be
in an unusually jovial mood and if he didn't actually
beam at Paddington at least his lips cracked in something approaching a smile as he looked over the fence.

'Did you enjoy your trip to Peru, bear?' he asked.

'Yes, thank you, Mr Curry,' said Paddington earnestly.

The Browns' neighbour waved a large mallet in
Paddington's direction. 'I wonder if you'd care to
lend a paw, bear,' he said casually. 'I'm putting in
some stakes and it's a bit difficult with only one pair
of hands.'

Mr Curry's voice droned on about his various jobs as he helped Paddington through a hole in the fence.

'Now, I've marked the positions where I want them all,' he continued as Paddington stood up. 'There are one hundred and fifty altogether. I'll just show you what I want done and then you can carry on while I go out and do my shopping. I want to get some paint for my new serving hatch when it's in.'

Mr Curry paused for breath. 'I don't suppose you'll get all the stakes in before I'm back, but if you do you can collect some rubble for me. It's for the foundations and I'm running a bit short. In fact, I might even give you sixpence if you do.'

'Mind you,' he added, before Paddington had time to speak, 'I shan't if it's not proper brick rubble. I don't want to come back home and find half my rockery missing.'

'Now, come along, bear,' he growled sternly, as he handed Paddington the mallet. 'Don't just stand there. I've got a lot of shopping to do and I want to get out this morning.'

Mr Curry picked up a stake from a nearby pile and then pushed it firmly into the ground with both hands. 'Now,' he said, 'when I nod my head, you hit it.'

For a moment Paddington looked at Mr Curry as if he could hardly believe his ears and then, as the Browns' neighbour closed his eyes and began nodding his head vigorously to show that he was ready, he took a firm grasp of the mallet with both paws.

A moment later a yell of pain rang out round Windsor Gardens, echoing and re-echoing in and out of the buildings.

Paddington jumped back in alarm and the mallet fell unheeded from his paws as to his surprise, instead of looking pleased, Mr Curry let go of the stake, gave another tremendous yell, and then began dancing up and down clutching his head with both hands.

'Bear!' he roared, as Paddington disappeared through the hole in the fence. 'Bear! Where are you, bear? Come back, bear!'

But Paddington was nowhere to be seen. Only the faintest movement of the raspberry canes betrayed his whereabouts, and a few moments later even that stopped as Mr Curry peered over the fence before staggering back up the garden towards his house.

For the next few minutes the distant sound of banging doors and the hiss of running water greeted Paddington's ears, but at long last a final and much louder bang from the front of Mr Curry's house caused him to heave a sigh of relief as he stood up and brushed himself clean.

Paddington hesitated for a moment and then climbed back through the hole in the fence and stared gloomily at the beginnings of Mr Curry's path.

The Browns' neighbour had a habit of twisting words so that his listeners were never quite certain

what had actually been said, but he was almost sure he hadn't agreed to lend a paw with *one* of the stakes let alone do all one hundred and fifty by himself.

Now that he had time to examine it more carefully the pile of stakes looked even bigger than it had at first sight. Not only that, but to add to his troubles Mr Curry appeared to have taken the mallet away with him.

After making several attempts to knock in some stakes with the aid of half a brick Paddington gave up in disgust and hurried up the path in the direction of Mr Curry's house.

In his haste the Browns' neighbour had left his back door ajar and a few moments later Paddington let himself cautiously into the kitchen.

The curtains were drawn and as he blinked in order to accustom his eyes to the change of light Paddington suddenly stopped in his tracks and stared in astonishment, all thoughts of the missing mallet driven from his mind.

It was some while since he'd last set foot in Mr Curry's kitchen and from the little he could remember of it the decorations then had been mostly of a rather dirty brown colour, certainly nothing like the ones which greeted him now.

In fact, all in all, apart from a bag of tools in one corner and one or two obviously unfinished patches it now looked not unlike something out of one of Mrs Brown's glossy magazines, or even, for that matter, Mrs Brown's own freshly decorated kitchen itself. The walls were gleaming white, the floor black and equally shiny, and even the stove and the refrigerator looked new.

It was as he stood taking it all in that a thoughtful expression gradually came over Paddington's face. Leaning against one of the walls was a wooden frame and a pair of doors and seeing it reminded him of a remark passed by Mr Curry as he'd helped him through the fence.

'I'm on the last lap in my kitchen, bear,' he'd said. 'There's only the serving hatch to put in and the job will be done.'

Mr Curry had gone on to grumble about the number of unfinished jobs he had on hand but at the time Paddington had been too busy worrying about the stakes to take much notice. However, the more he thought about the matter now the more it seemed like a golden opportunity to make amends for the unfortunate accident earlier in the day.

A few minutes later the sound of hammering could be heard in Windsor Gardens. It was followed shortly afterwards by the dull thud of a falling brick, the first of many which gradually found their way from inside the kitchen to a large pile outside the back door.

Paddington felt sure from the little Mr Curry had said about all his jobs that he couldn't fail to be pleased if he arrived home later that morning and found his serving hatch already installed. And even if the hatch itself wasn't in place he couldn't possibly find anything to grumble at in having a start made on the hole.

Apart from that, knocking down walls was much more enjoyable work than banging in stakes. Once a start had been made by removing the first brick, which

had taken rather a lot of hammering with a cold-chisel, it was more a matter of clouting everything in sight as hard as possible, and standing back every now and then to avoid being hit by some of the larger lumps as they parted company from the rest.

Soon the air was so thick with dust it became almost impossible to see, but as the last brick fell to the floor Paddington surveyed the result of his labours as best he could through half-closed eyes and then measured the space carefully with his paws in order to make sure it was the right size.

After placing the frame carefully into position and making it secure by jamming a couple of pieces of wood either side, he slipped the doors into their grooves and then stood back waiting for the dust to settle so that he could inspect his handiwork.

As the air gradually cleared Paddington began to look more and more pleased with himself. Admittedly the hatch wasn't perfectly level, and there were one or two rather unfortunate paw marks on the surrounding wall, but those two things apart he decided it was one of the best jobs he could ever remember doing and he felt sure Mr Curry would be equally pleased when he saw it.

Dipping his paw into a nearby jar of marmalade he idly pushed one of the doors to one side in order to make sure it slid properly on its runners.

As he did so the pleased expression suddenly drained from Paddington's face and he nearly toppled over backwards with surprise as he took in the view through the open hatch.

Since he'd lived with the Browns he'd examined number thirty-two Windsor Gardens from a good many different angles but never in his wildest dreams had he ever pictured seeing it through a serving hatch in Mr Curry's kitchen wall, particularly when he'd expected to see a dining-room instead.

For a moment Paddington stood where he was with his feet frozen to the ground and then he hurried outside rubbing his eyes in order to make sure it wasn't all part of some terrible dream.

As he peered up at the outside wall, Paddington's worst fears were realised and gradually the truth of

the matter dawned on him. In his hurry to complete the job he'd quite forgotten the fact that although Mr Curry's house was exactly the same in most respects as the Browns', because it was next door everything was the other way round, so that what was the dining-room wall in the Browns' house became the outside wall in Mr Curry's.

Paddington's face grew longer and longer as he considered the matter. According to Mrs Bird, Mr Curry had been doing quite a few jobs in his house of late but for the life of him he couldn't think of a single good reason why he would possibly want a serving hatch in his outside wall.

There were still several pieces of brick lying on the ground where they had fallen, but after one or two attempts he soon gave up all hope of fitting them back into position.

How long he stayed lost in thought Paddington wasn't quite sure, but he was suddenly roused from his day-dreams by the sound of Mr Curry's side gate banging shut.

Hurrying round to the back of the house he was just in time to meet the Browns' neighbour coming round the other way. Apart from some sticking plaster on the back of his head, Mr Curry looked little the worse for his earlier encounter with Paddington. Nevertheless his face darkened as they bumped into each other.

'What are you up to now, bear?' he growled.

'What am I up to, Mr Curry?' said Paddington, playing for time.

Mr Curry looked suspiciously at the brick dust sticking to Paddington's fur and then, as he caught sight
of the pile of brick rubble outside the kitchen door, his
face suddenly cleared.

'Good work, bear,' he said approvingly, as he felt in
his pocket. 'I promised you sixpence and I must say
you've earned it.'

'Thank you very much, Mr Curry,' said Paddington doubtfully, as he took the coin. 'I'll keep it for a
while in case you want it back.'

'What!' exclaimed Mr Curry. 'Nonsense! Of course
I shan't want it back. This rubble's just what I need for
my path.'

'I don't think I should use it for your path, Mr
Curry,' said Paddington anxiously. 'You may want it
for something else.'

Mr Curry gave a loud snort as he picked up his
shovel. 'Not use it,' he repeated. 'Give me one good
reason why I shouldn't, bear.'

Paddington looked on unhappily as Mr Curry transferred the pile of rubble into a nearby trench and when,
some while later, the Browns' neighbour poured a
barrowload of wet cement over the top, he looked
unhappier still.

'There!' said Mr Curry, rubbing his hands together.
'That won't come up again in a hurry once it's set.' He
turned, but for the second time that morning found
himself addressing the empty air, for his audience, like

the brick rubble, had completely disappeared from view.

Paddington felt sure he could give the Browns' neighbour not one, but several very good reasons why he shouldn't have used the bricks he'd found outside his kitchen door. On the other hand he was equally sure he would be much happier if Mr Curry discovered the reasons for himself, perferably some time in the dim and distant future, and certainly when the cause of it all was a long, long way away.

Paddington sat up in bed holding a thermometer in his paw. 'I think I must have caught the measles, Mrs Bird,' he announced weakly. 'My temperature's over one hundred and twenty!'

'One hundred and twenty!' Mrs Bird hurriedly examined the thermometer. 'That's not a temperature,' she exclaimed with relief. 'That's a marmalade stain.'

Mrs Brown looked Paddington over carefully. 'He's certainly got some red spots on him,' she said. 'It's a bit difficult to tell with fur, but I suppose it could be measles.'

'Hmm,' said Mrs Bird suspiciously. 'That's as may be. But it's the first time I've ever known measles spots come off on the sheets.'

'Perhaps they've worked loose, Mrs Bird,' said Paddington hopefully. 'I've been scratching them.'

Mrs Brown exchanged a glance with her housekeeper. 'It looks more like brick dust to me,' she said.

Mrs Bird glanced out of the window towards the house next door. 'Talking of brick dust,' she said, 'reminds me that Mr Curry called to see you just now, Paddington.'

'Oh, dear,' said Mrs Brown, as a loud groan came from the direction of Paddington's bed. 'Is anything the matter?'

'I think I've had a bit of a relapse, Mrs Brown,' said a weak voice from under the sheet. 'I don't think I ought to do any more talking.'

'That's a pity,' said Mrs Bird. 'He asked me to give you sixpence.'

'Sixpence!' exclaimed Paddington, sitting up in bed suddenly. 'But I've already had *one*.'

'In that case,' said Mrs Bird, 'you've got a shilling.'

'Apparently he's very pleased with his new delivery hatch,' explained Mrs Brown. 'All sorts of people have been congratulating him. The milkman. The baker. The boy from the grocery shop. They all think it's a splendid idea. Mr Curry's going to build a cupboard inside so that they can leave things and he won't have to answer the door.'

'There'll be no holding him now he's got something no one else has thought of,' said Mrs Bird. 'He'll be like a dog with two tails. You mark my words, we shall hear of nothing else from morning to night.'

'It certainly is a good idea,' said Mrs Brown, as she paused at the door. 'Mind you,' she continued, 'I can't help feeling it's a good job Judy managed to catch the milkman when she did.'

'And that Jonathan had a chat with the baker,' added Mrs Bird.

'Otherwise,' said Mrs Brown, 'I might not have thought to have a word with the grocery boy.'

'And where,' said her housekeeper, 'would we have been then?'

Mrs Bird looked towards Paddington's bed but the only answer she received was a loud groan as its occupant appeared to have another sudden relapse.

All the same, although as groans went it was a long and rather blood-curdling one, there was something about the set of Paddington's whiskers as they poked out from beneath the sheets which somehow managed to suggest the possibility of a recovery in the not-too-distant future.

'I give it until tea-time at the outside,' said Mrs Brown, as she closed the door.

'If not before,' agreed Mrs Bird. 'I'm baking a treacle tart for tea.'

'In that case,' said Mrs Brown, 'definitely before. There's nothing like a few whiffs of treacle tart up the stairs for curing even the worst attack of a young bear's measles!'

6.
Too Much off the Top

Paddington's friend, Mr Gruber, chuckled to himself when he heard about Mr Curry's delivery hatch the next day.

'What a good thing it turned out all right in the end, Mr Brown,' he said, as they settled themselves in the deck-chairs on the pavement outside his shop together with a tray of buns and two steaming mugs of cocoa. 'Although I must say it would have served Mr Curry right if it hadn't. It might have taught him not to go taking advantage of others quite so much.

'Mind you, Mr Brown,' he continued, 'it's very difficult to get help these days so I suppose we shouldn't be too hard on him.'

Mr Gruber shook his head sadly. 'You'd be surprised if I told you some of the trouble I've had just lately. If you don't get help, people just won't bother to wait. And if you get the wrong sort of help it frightens the customers away. This is our busy season too. Especially with all the American tourists over here for their holidays.'

Mr Gruber went on to explain that English antiques of almost any shape or form were very popular in the United States and that apart from the tourists some dealers came over simply to buy up as many as possible.

He waved his hand at all the gleaming copper pots and pans, vases, books, ornaments, and other bric-à-brac which lined the walls of his shop and overflowed out on the pavement.

'I must say I've missed your help, Mr Brown,' he said. 'Apart from the pleasure of our little chats, one young bear with a knowledge of antiques and an eye for a bargain is worth his weight in gold.'

Mr Gruber disappeared into his shop for a moment and when he returned he was carrying an old vase. 'What would you say this is, Mr Brown?' he asked casually, holding it up to the light.

Paddington looked most surprised at such a simple question. 'That's an early Spode, Mr Gruber,' he replied promptly.

Mr Gruber nodded his approval. 'Exactly,' he said. 'But you'd be surprised how many people wouldn't realise it.'

'Do you know, Mr Brown, one young man I had working here while you were away actually called it a *jug* and he was going to let it go for fourpence simply because it had this piece missing. I only just rescued it in time.'

Mr Gruber fell silent as he fitted the broken piece of china back into the vase and Paddington nearly fell off his deck-chair with surprise at the thought of there being people in the world who didn't know about antique pottery and how valuable it could be. 'Four-pence for a Spode!' he exclaimed, hardly able to believe his ears.

'Mind you,' said Mr Gruber, 'let's be fair. Not every-one has your advantage, Mr Brown. After all, you've spent so much time in this shop I believe you know almost as much about it as I do. If you ever decide to go into business a lot of people will have to look to their laurels.'

Paddington looked pleased at his friend's remarks. Mr Gruber wasn't in the habit of paying idle compli-ments and praise from him was praise indeed.

'Perhaps I could help by repairing that vase for you, Mr Gruber,' he offered.

Mr Gruber looked at him doubtfully over the top of his glasses. Although he had a high regard for Pad-dington and had meant every word he'd said, he also knew that accidents could happen in the best-regulated circles, especially bears' circles. However, he was a kindly man at heart and after a moment's thought he nodded his agreement.

'It's very kind of you, Mr Brown,' he said. 'I know you'll take great care of it, but don't forget "there's many a slip 'twixt cup and lip".'

'I won't, Mr Gruber,' said Paddington, as he took the vase and its broken piece and laid it carefully amongst some cabbages in the bottom of his shopping basket on wheels.

After Mr Gruber had sorted out some money for a tube of glue from a nearby stationer's, Paddington waved good-bye and hurried off up the road with a thoughtful expression on his face.

Although he hadn't said much about it he was still feeling very upset by the business of the forged oil share. Apart from the feeling of having a fortune slip through his paws there was the matter of losing a day's interest through not putting the change from his presents straight in the bank and he was anxious to make it up in some way.

Mr Gruber's chance remark about going into business had suddenly reminded him of a notice which he'd seen in a shop window that very morning.

At the time he hadn't given it a great deal of attention, but now, as he reached the shop and stood looking at it again, he began to look more and more interested.

The shop, which was surmounted by a long striped pole, had the words. S. SLOOP – GENT'S HAIRDRESSING emblazoned across the door and the notice in the window said, quite simply, WILLING JUNIOR WANTED – URGENTLY.

Underneath, in rough capitals, Mr Sloop had added the information that a good wage would be paid to any keen young lad willing to learn the trade.

Paddington stood for quite some while breathing heavily on the glass until he suddenly became aware of a face on the other side watching him with equal interest.

Taking his courage in both paws Paddington pushed open the door of the shop, dragging his shopping basket after him, and raised his hat as he bade the owner good morning.

' 'Morning,' replied Mr Sloop breezily, reaching for a white cloth. 'What can I do for you? Short back and sides, or would you like one of our "all-in specials"? Haircut, shampoo, and set – all for five bob. Tell you what – seeing trade's a bit slack this morning – I'll give you special bear rates – you can have the lot for three and six.'

Paddington stepped back hastily as Mr Sloop waved a pair of clippers dangerously close to his head. 'I haven't come for a haircut,' he explained, placing his hat firmly back over his ears. 'I've come about the job.'

'You've *what*?' Mr Sloop lost some of his breeziness as he stared at Paddington.

'It says in the window you want a willing junior,' said Paddington hopefully.

'Blimey!' Mr Sloop stood back and examined Paddington. 'You wouldn't be a very good advertisement, I must say. This is a barber's shop, not an art school. I'd have to whip all them whiskers off for a start.'

'Whip my whiskers off!' exclaimed Paddington hotly. 'But I've always had them.'

Mr Sloop considered the matter for a moment. 'I suppose I could stand you in the window like one of them "before and after" advertisements,' he said grudgingly. 'Not that I'm saying "yes", mind. But I don't mind admitting I've been let down badly by the Labour Exchange. Nobody wants to sweep up hairs these days.'

'Bears are good at sweeping,' said Paddington eagerly. 'I don't think I've done any hairs before but I often help Mrs Bird in the mornings.'

'Errands,' said Mr Sloop. 'There'll be lots of errands to run. And you'll have to look after things when I pop out for me morning coffee. Keep the customers happy till I get back. Then there's the shop to keep clean. It's not so bad in the week – it's Saturday mornings. The steam fair rises off me scissors on a Saturday morning.'

Mr Sloop mopped his brow at the thought as he gave Paddington a sidelong glance. 'Some people might consider it a lot of work for . . . er . . . thirty bob a week.'

'Thirty shillings!' exclaimed Paddington, nearly falling over backwards at the thought of so much money. '*Every* week. That's over a hundred buns!'

'Done, then,' said Mr Sloop, hurriedly coming to a decision before Paddington could change his mind.

'Mind you,' he added, 'it's only a trial. And no reading comics on the sly when me back's turned. But if you watch points and don't get up to any tricks, I might even let you have a go with the clippers in a week or so.'

'Thank you very much, Mr Sloop,' said Paddington gratefully. In the past he had often peered through the barber shop window and watched Mr Sloop run his clippers round the necks of his customers and the thought of actually being allowed to have a go filled him with excitement.

Mr Sloop clapped his hands together briskly and licked his lips. 'No time like the present,' he said. 'I could do with a coffee right now. May as well take advantage of the lull, as you might say. You'll find a broom in that cupboard over there. When you've done the floor you can give the basins a going over – only mind them razors – don't go nicking yer paws. I don't want no bear's blood all over the place – it'll give the shop a bad name.'

Having finished his instructions Mr Sloop added that he wouldn't be long and then disappeared out of the door leaving Paddington standing in the middle of the shop with a slightly bemused expression on his face.

Cutting hair seemed much more complicated than it looked at first sight, and Mr Sloop's shop, though it was only small, appeared to have almost as many things inside it as a supermarket.

Along one wall was a row of several benches for customers, together with a pile of newspapers for them to read while they were waiting, and pinned to the wall behind them were a number of pictures cut from magazines showing the various styles it was possible to have.

The back of the shop was given over to a large cupboard and a number of notices. Mr Sloop didn't appear to have a great deal of trust in his fellow human beings for most of them were to do with payment and the fact that under no circumstances would any cheques be cashed or credit given.

But it was the business side of the room, where the chair itself stood, that aroused Paddington's immediate interest. Almost the whole of the wall was taken up by a long mirror and on a shelf in front of the mirror stood row upon row of bottles. There were bottles of hair-oil, shampoo, setting lotion, hair restorer, cream, the list was endless and Paddington spent several minutes unscrewing caps in order to sniff the contents of the various bottles.

It wasn't until he was having a practice snip with a pair of scissors and narrowly missed cutting off one of his own whiskers that Paddington suddenly came back to earth with a bump and realised that he hadn't even started work. He hurried across to the cupboard and opened the door only to be met by a positive deluge of old brooms and brushes, not to mention white coats, towels, and various other items.

As far as he could see, Mr Sloop must have been without any help in his shop for some while, for most of the things were so tangled together it took him all his time to find out which handle belonged to which broom let alone decide on the one to use.

It was when the confusion was at its height that Paddington vaguely heard a bell ringing and from his position in the back of the cupboard he suddenly realised that someone in the shop was carrying on a conversation.

'Say, do I get any service in this place?' called a voice with a strong American accent from the direction of Mr Sloop's chair.

Paddington scrambled out of the cupboard and peered across the room to where the owner of the voice lay waiting with his arms folded and his eyes closed.

'I'd like a trim, please,' announced the man as he heard the commotion going on behind him. 'Not too little – not too much – and don't touch the top. Make it snappy. I have a plane to catch later on and I have a lot of packing to do.'

'Look,' continued the voice impatiently, as Paddington hurried across the shop and peered hopefully out through the open door in search of Mr Sloop, 'this *is* a barber's shop, isn't it? Do I get my hair cut or don't I? All I want is to get back to my hotel so as I can make up on some sleep before I catch my plane. I'm that tired. I've been on my feet for a week now ...'

The man's voice trailed away into a loud yawn and to Paddington's astonishment as he turned back into the shop he was greeted, not by a string of further complaints as he'd expected, but by a long, gentle snore.

Paddington had seen some people go to sleep quickly before, Mr Brown in particular on a Sunday afternoon was often very quick, but he'd never seen it happen quite so suddenly. He stood in the middle of the shop for a moment looking anxiously at the figure in Mr Sloop's chair and then gradually the expression on his face was replaced by one of interest.

Although the man in the chair had obviously dozed off for the moment he'd certainly been in a great hurry. In fact, he'd definitely said to make it snappy. And although Mr Sloop hadn't actually said he could cut anyone's hair that very day he had mentioned something about having a go at a later date and he'd also said that one of Paddington's first jobs would be to keep the cusomers happy.

As far as Paddington could see, about the only thing that would make Mr Sloop's present customer happy would be if he were to wake up and find his hair had been cut while he'd been asleep.

After giving the matter several moments' more thought, Paddington came to a decision. Taking care not to disturb the sleeping figure, he draped a white cloth round the man's shoulders and then picked up Mr Sloop's electric clippers which were hanging from a nearby hook.

After giving a few practice waves through the air in order to get used to the tickling sensation they made when they were switched on, Paddington applied the business end carefully to the back of the man's neck, making a wide sweeping movement with his paw as he'd often seen Mr Sloop do in the past.

The first stroke was rather disappointing. It went much deeper than he had intended and left a long white path up the back of the neck. The second stroke, on the other hand, didn't go nearly as deep so that he had to spend several minutes trying to match the two, and he cast some anxious glances over his shoulder in case Mr Sloop returned before he could repair the damage.

In fact, for the next minute or so, Paddington spent almost as much time looking out of the window as he did looking at the job in hand. When he did finally give his undivided attention to the figure in the chair his eyes nearly popped out of their sockets with astonishment.

The clippers dropped from his paw and he stood rooted to the spot as he stared at the top of the man's head. Before he'd started work it had been covered by a mass of thick black hair, whereas now, apart from a fringe round the ears and neck, it was almost completely bald.

The strange thing was it must all have happened in the blink of an eyelid for quite definitely the hair had been there when he'd looked a second before.

It was all most mysterious and Paddington sat down on his suitcase with a mournful expression on his face while he considered the matter. He was beginning to regret not having asked for his wages in advance for the more he thought about things the more difficult it became to picture Mr Sloop paying for one day's work let alone a week's.

It was while he was sitting on his suitcase that he suddenly caught sight of a bottle on a shelf above his head. It was a large bottle and it had a picture on the outside which showed a group of men, all with a luxuriant growth of jet black hair. But it wasn't so much the picture which caught his eye as the words underneath, which said, in large red letters: DR SPOONER'S QUICK ACTION MAGIC HAIR RESTORER.

Paddington was a hopeful bear in many ways but after using up several spoons of the thick yellow liquid even he began to admit to himself that he might be asking a little too much of Dr Spooner's tonic. Looking through his binoculars didn't help matters either for the top of the man's head remained as shiny and hairless as ever.

He was just toying desperately with the idea of buying some quick drying black paint from a nearby hardware store in order to cover up the worst of the damage when his eye alighted on his shopping basket on wheels which was standing in a corner of the shop and an excited gleam came into his eyes.

Carefully lifting out Mr Gruber's vase, which he placed on a shelf in front of the chair for safety, Paddington rummaged around in the basket until he found what he was looking for.

Although Mr Gruber had asked him to buy the glue for the express purpose of mending the vase,

Paddington felt sure he wouldn't mind if it was used for something else in an emergency, and as far as he could see this was definitely one of the worst emergencies he had ever encountered.

For the next few minutes Paddington was very busy. Having squeezed drops of Mr Gruber's glue all over the man's head, he then rummaged around on the floor in search of some hair to fill in the vacant spot.

Fortunately, being short of an assistant, Mr Sloop hadn't bothered to sweep up that morning and so there was quite a selection to choose from.

At long last Paddington stood back, and examined his handiwork with interest. All in all, he felt quite pleased with himself. Admittedly the top of the man's head had undergone a somewhat drastic change since he'd first sat in the chair – for one thing there were now quite a number of ginger curls, not to mention blonde streaks, in the long straight black bits – and several of them were sticking out at a rather odd angle – but at least it was all covered and he heaved a sigh of relief as he wiped his paws on the cloth in front of him.

It was as he was pushing a particularly springy ginger curl into place with his paw as a final touch that to his alarm the figure in the chair began to stir.

Paddington hurried round the other side of the chair and stood between Mr Sloop's customer and the mirror.

'That'll be three and six, please,' he said, holding out his paw hopefully in a business-like manner as he consulted the price list on the wall.

If the man looked surprised at the sight of Paddington's paw under his nose, it was nothing compared with the expression which came over his face a moment later as he caught sight of his reflection in the mirror.

Jumping out of the chair, he pushed Paddington to one side and stood for a moment staring at the sight which met his eyes. For a second or two he seemed speechless and then he let out a roar of rage as he made a grab for the nearest object to hand.

Paddington's own look of alarm changed to one of horror as the man picked up the vase from the shelf and made as if to dash it to the ground.

'Look out!' he cried anxiously. 'That's Mr Gruber's Spode.'

To Paddington's suprise his words had a far greater effect than he'd expected for the man suddenly froze in mid-air, lowered his arms and then stared at the object in front of him with a look of disbelief.

'Thank you very much,' said Paddington gratefully, as he withdrew the vase from the man's hands and placed it carefully in his shopping basket on wheels. 'It's got a piece missing already and I don't think Mr Gruber would like it very much if the rest was broken.'

'Perhaps you'd like to break one of Mr Sloop's bottles instead,' he added generously. 'He's got some old ones in the cupboard.'

The man took a deep breath, looked at himself once again in the mirror, passed a trembling hand over his brow and then turned back to Paddington.

'Now see here, bear,' he said. 'I don't know what's been going on. Maybe it's all part of a bad dream, maybe I'm gonna wake up in a minute, but this Mr Gruber – he's a friend of yours?'

'He's my special friend,' said Paddington import-

antly. 'We have buns and cocoa together every morning.'

'And this is the Spode?' asked the man.

'Yes,' said Paddington in surprise. 'He's got lots. He
keeps an antique shop and . . .'

'Lead me to him, bear,' said the man warmly. 'Just
lead me to him.'

Mr Gruber took one last look out of his door to make
sure everything was in for the night and then turned
back to Paddington.

'You know, Mr Brown,' he said, as they settled
themselves on the horsehair sofa at the back of the
shop, 'I still can't believe it. I really can't.'

Paddington, nodding from behind a cloud of cocoa

steam, looked very much as if he agreed with every word.

'If anyone mentions the word "coincidence" to me again,' continued Mr Gruber, 'I shall always tell them the story of the day you got a job as a hairdresser and knocked the toupee off an American antique dealer's head.'

'I thought I'd cut all his hair off by mistake, Mr Gruber,' admitted Paddington.

Mr Gruber chuckled at the thought. 'I shouldn't like to have been in your paws if you really had, Mr Brown.'

'Fancy,' he continued, 'if you hadn't knocked his toupee off and put all that glue on his head he wouldn't have got cross. And if you hadn't put my Spode on the shelf he wouldn't have heard about my shop. And if he hadn't heard about my shop he would have gone back to America to-night without half the things he came over to buy. It's what they call a chain of events, Mr Brown, and a very good day's work into the bargain. I can see I shall have to go to a few more sales to make up for all the empty spaces on my shelves.'

Paddington looked out through the window and then sniffed the warm air from the stove. Most of the other shops in the Portobello Road already had their shutters up and even those that were still open showed signs of closing for the night as one by one their lights went out.

'And if all those things hadn't happened, Mr Gruber,'

he said, as he reached across for the earthenware jug, 'we shouldn't be sitting here now.'

Paddington always enjoyed his cups of cocoa with Mr Gruber, but it was most unusual to have one together so late in the day and he was anxious to make the most of it.

Mr Gruber nodded his head in agreement. 'And that, if I may say so, Mr Brown,' he said warmly, 'is the nicest link of all.'

7.
Paddington
Steps Out

Mrs Brown looked out of the car window. 'If you want my opinion,' she said, lowering her voice so that the occupants of the back seat, and one occupant in particular, shouldn't hear, 'bringing Paddington with us is asking for trouble. You know what happened when he went to Jonathan's school.'

'That wasn't exactly a disaster,' said Mr Brown mildly. 'If I remember rightly he saved the day. If it hadn't been for him the old boys would never have won their cricket match.'

'Playing in a cricket match isn't the same as watching ballet,' replied Mrs Brown. 'He'll never sit quietly through a whole afternoon of it. Something's bound to happen.'

She gave a sigh. Ever since Paddington had taken part in an epic cricket match at Jonathan's school,

Judy had been clamouring for him to visit her school in turn and Mrs Brown knew that she was fighting a losing battle.

Having a bear in the family gave both Jonathan and Judy a certain amount of prestige amongst their fellow pupils and Judy was anxious to catch up on the lead at present held by her brother. All the same, as they drew nearer and nearer to Judy's school, Mrs Brown began to look more and more worried.

'Good heavens!' exclaimed Mr Brown suddenly as they turned a corner and passed through some wrought iron gates let into a grey stone wall. He waved his hand towards a seething mass of girls in uniform as he brought the car to a halt. 'What's this – some sort of reception committee?'

'What did I tell you?' said Mrs Brown, as the familiar figure of Judy detached itself from the crowd and came forward to greet them. 'It's started already.'

'Nonsense!' said Mr Brown. All the same he cast some anxious glances towards the paintwork on his car as he helped the others out and exchanged greetings with his daughter.

Paddington, as he clambered out of the back seat, looked even more surprised as he stood blinking in the strong sunlight listening to the cheers, and he raised his hat several times in response to the cries.

'Come along, Paddington,' said Judy, grabbing his paw. 'You've lots of people to meet *and* we've got to pay a visit to the tuck shop. I told Mrs Beedle, the lady in charge, all about you and she's laid on some special marmalade sandwiches.'

'Mrs Beedle's laid on some marmalade sandwiches!' exclaimed Paddington, looking most impressed. Although he was very keen on anything to do with marmalade and had several times sat on a sandwich by mistake he'd never met anyone who'd actually done it on purpose before, particularly someone in charge of a tuck shop. However, before he had time to inquire into the matter the throng of girls closed in behind him and he felt himself being propelled gently but firmly in the direction of a small building which stood to one side of the quadrangle in front of the main block.

As the milling crowd of figures disappeared through the door of the tuck shop, Mrs Brown looked towards a large, brightly coloured poster on a board near the main gate. 'I thought this Russian dancer they're having down – Sergei Oblomov – was supposed to be the guest of honour,' she remarked. 'I don't think he'll like it if he turns up and there's no one here. I'm sure all these girls were meant for him, not Paddington.'

'Talk of the devil,' said Mr Brown, as a large important looking black car swept in through the gates and came to a halt a few yards away. 'I have a feeling this *is* him.'

Pretending to study the scenery, the Browns nevertheless watched with interest as the door of the car opened and a tall figure dressed in a black cloak alighted and stood for a moment with one hand in the air looking expectantly all around.

'Crikey!' said Jonathan a few moments later as the sound of a door being slammed echoed round the quadrangle and the car swept past them in a cloud of dust towards the school building. 'He didn't look in a very good mood.'

'Black as ink,' agreed Mr Brown. 'It wasn't exactly what you might call a good entrance. Not so much as a pigeon cooed.'

'I don't suppose you'd like it,' said Mrs Brown, 'if you were a famous dancer and you had your thunder stolen by a bear. Especially one stuffing himself with marmalade sandwiches in a school tuck shop.'

'He doesn't know it's a bear,' reasoned Mr Brown. 'He's never even met Paddington.'

'No,' said Mrs Brown decidely, as they made their way towards the school building, 'he hasn't. And if I have my way he's not going to either.'

She cast some anxious glances in the direction of the tuck shop as they passed by. Several times the ominous sound of cheering had come from the open windows and one or two of them had been decidedly loud, rather as if things were getting out of control.

All the same, as they seated themselves in the school hall some while later, even Mrs Brown found it hard to fault Paddington's appearance. Admittedly there were still one or two traces of marmalade on his whiskers and his fur had lost some of its smooth sheen, but all in all he looked unusually well behaved as he settled himself at the end of the row by the gangway and examined his programme with interest.

'You know, I'm really looking forward to this,' said Mrs Bird with enthusiasm, as she made herself comfortable. 'I like ballet dancing.'

The others looked at their housekeeper in surprise as a far-away look came into her eyes. 'I haven't seen any good dancing for I don't know how many years.'

'I'm not sure you're going to now,' whispered Mr Brown, as the curtain rose to reveal a woodland glade and several small figures dressed as toadstools.

'It's the Juniors,' whispered Judy. 'They're doing their "nature" dance.'

Paddington opened his suitcase, took out his opera glasses, and peered at the stage with interest.

'Are you enjoying it?' whispered Judy.

Paddington thought for a moment. 'It's all right,' he announced after some thought. 'But I can't hear what they're saying.'

'People don't *say* anything in ballet,' hissed Judy. 'They mime it all. You have to guess what they're doing by the dancing.'

Paddington sank back into his seat. Although he didn't want to hurt Judy's feelings by saying so, he didn't think much of ballet at all. As far as he could see it was just a lot of people running after each other on the stage, and apart from not saying anything, which made it all rather difficult to follow, he began to wonder why they didn't get taller dancers in the first place as some of the older girls in particular seemed to spend most of the time standing on their toes. However, he was a polite bear and he applauded dutifully at the end of each item.

'I must say that swan took a long time to die,' said Mr Brown, as the lights went up at long last to herald the interval. 'I thought she was never going to get it over with.'

'I liked the flying ballet,' said Mrs Brown, amid general agreement. 'I thought that was very well done.'

'I'd like to go up in the air on a wire like that,' said Jonathan. 'I bet it's super.'

Judy handed Paddington her programme. 'It's the famous Russian dancer next,' she said. 'Look – there's his picture.'

Paddington peered at the programme with interest. 'Surge Oblomov!' he exclaimed in surprise.

'It's not *Surge*,' said Judy. 'It's pronounced Sur-guy.'

'Sir Guy Oblomov,' repeated Paddington, looking most impressed as he studied the picture. 'I don't think I've ever seen a Lord doing a ballet dance before.'

'He isn't a Lord – he's a . . .' Judy gave a sigh as she sought for the right words. Sometimes explaining things to Paddington became complicated out of all proportion.

'Well, whatever he is,' said Mrs Bird, coming to her rescue, 'I'm really looking forward to it. It's a great treat.'

'Oh, crikey!' exclaimed Judy suddenly, as a girl

from the row behind whispered something in her ear.
'I'm not sure if he's going to appear after all. They're
having some trouble back stage.'

'What!' exclaimed Paddington hotly. 'Sir Guy
Oblomov's not going to appear!'

'Oh, dear,' said Mrs Bird. 'How very disappointing.'

Paddington stared at the drawn curtains on the stage
hardly able to believe his ears as everyone began talking at once. Judy's words had reached several other
people near by and soon a buzz of excitement went
round the hall.

'It's something to do with no one being at the gates
to meet him,' explained the girl in the seat behind.
'He's a bit temperamental and it upset him rather.'

Mr and Mrs Brown exchanged glances. 'I told you
so, Henry,' said Mrs Brown. 'I said if we brought
Paddington something would happen.'

'Well, you can't really blame poor old Paddington
for this,' replied Mr Brown indignantly. 'It's not his
fault if everyone wanted to meet him instead of some
blessed ballet dancer chap. After all . . .' Mr Brown
suddenly broke off in mid-sentence. 'That's funny,' he
said, as he looked along the aisle. 'Talking of Paddington, where's he got to?'

'He was here a second ago,' said Judy, looking all
around.

'Look!' cried Jonathan, pointing down the aisle.
'There he is!'

The Browns followed the direction of Jonathan's

arm and were just in time to see a small figure disappear through a door at the side of the stage. From where they were sitting it wasn't possible to see the expression on Paddington's face but there was a determined slant to his hat and a look about his duffle coat which seemed to bode ill for anyone who got in his way.

'Don't you think you'd better go after him, Judy?' said Mrs Brown anxiously.

'Too late,' groaned Judy. 'Did you see who was behind the door? Miss Grimshaw!'

Judy sank lower and lower into her seat as she contemplated the awful prospect of Paddington coming face to face with her headmistress, although had she but known, Miss Grimshaw, weighed down by all the worries back stage, seemed almost glad to find someone from outside the school she could talk to.

'Are you Russian?' she asked hopefully, after Paddington had introduced himself.

'Well, I am in a bit of a hurry,' admitted Paddington, raising his hat politely. 'I've come to see Sir Guy.'

Miss Grimshaw looked at him suspiciously. 'I said "Russian",' she explained. 'Not *rushing*. And I'm not at all sure Mr Oblomov will see you. I was hoping you might be Russian so that you could talk to him in his own language and make him feel more at home, but if you're not I'd rather you didn't.'

'Mrs Bird's very upset,' replied Paddington.

'I'm sure she is,' said Miss Grimshaw. 'I'm upset.

We're all upset. Mr Oblomov's upset. Deirdre Shaw's upset.'

'*Deirdre Shaw?*' echoed Paddington, looking most surprised.

'She was supposed to partner Mr Oblomov in the *Pas de deux*,' explained Miss Grimshaw. 'Then when Mr Oblomov said he wouldn't dance she ran off to her dormitory in tears and no-one's seen her since.'

While Miss Grimshaw was speaking, a nearby door opened and a tall, imposing figure in black tights emerged.

'I hov changed my mind,' announced Mr Oblomov, waving his hand imperiously as he did a series of knee-bending exercises. 'I will not disappoint my public. First I will dance my famous solo from the Swan Lake. Then I will perform the *Pas de deux*. I trust everything is ready, no?'

'No,' exclaimed Miss Grimshaw. 'I mean . . . that is to say . . . yes. I'm sure it will be.'

Miss Grimshaw's usual icy calm seemed to have deserted her for once as Sergei Oblomov strode past heading for the stage.

'Oh, dear,' she exclaimed. 'Now he's changed his mind *again* – and Deirdre Shaw's disappeared. What he's going to say when he finds he's without a partner in the second half I shudder to think.'

As the school orchestra started up and the curtain rose to a tremendous round of applause, Miss Grimshaw rushed off wringing her hands, leaving Paddington staring with a very thoughtful expression on his face indeed in the direction of the open door leading to Sergei Oblomov's dressing-room.

It was an expression that the Browns, had they been there, would have recognised immediately. But fortunately for their peace of mind they, like practically everyone else in the school, had their attention riveted to the stage.

Even Mr Brown sat up in his seat and clapped as loudly as anyone as Sergei Oblomov executed one perfect pirouette after another, spinning round and round so fast it left the audience breathless. And when he followed this with a series of breathtaking arabesques everyone gasped with admiration and the rafters of the hall fairly shook with the ovation which greeted the end of this item.

As the applause died away and Sergei Oblomov stood for a moment motionless in the beam from a single spotlight, Mrs Bird gave a quick glance at her programme. 'It's the *Pas de deux* now,' she whispered.

'Golly, I hope they've found Deidre Shaw,' said Judy in a low voice as the music started up. 'There's going to be an awful row if they haven't.'

'It's all right,' said Mr Brown. 'I think I can see someone lurking at the side of the stage.'

Judy followed the direction of Mr Brown's gaze and then jumped up from her seat in alarm.

'Crikey!' she exclaimed. 'That's not Deirdre Shaw. That's . . .'

'Paddington!' exclaimed the rest of the family, joining her in a chorus as the shadowy figure moved on to the stage and into the light.

'Mercy me!' cried Mrs Bird. 'What on earth is that bear up to now?'

Her words were lost in the gasp of astonishment which went up all around them as Paddington advanced towards the centre of the stage, placed his suitcase carefully in front of the footlights, and then raised his hat politely to the several members of the audience in the front row who began half-heartedly to applaud.

'Oh, dear, I wish he wouldn't wear that old hat,' said

Mrs Brown.

'And what on earth's he got on his legs?' asked Mrs Bird.

'Looks like some kind of sacking to me,' said Mr Brown.

'They're not sacks,' said Judy. 'They're tights.'

'Tights?' echoed Mr Brown. 'They don't look very tight to me. They look as if they're going to come down any moment.'

The Browns watched in horror as Paddington, having ventured one bow too many, hurriedly replaced his hat and grabbed hold of the roll of material which hung around his waist in large folds.

Now, for the first time since he'd decided to lend a paw with the ballet, he was beginning to wish he'd resisted the temptation to use the pair of tights which he'd found hanging on the back of Mr Oblomov's dressing-room door.

Bears' legs being rather short put him at a disadvantage to start with, but as far as he could make out Sergei Oblomov's legs were twice as long as anyone else's so that an unusually large amount of surplus material had to be lost at the top.

Apart from tying a piece of string round his waist Paddington had hopefully made use of several drawing pins which he'd found on a notice board at the back of the stage, but most of these seemed to have fallen out so he had to spend some moments making last minute adjustments to a large safety pin which he'd put on in case of an emergency.

It was at this moment that Sergei Oblomov, oblivious to all that had been going on, finished executing a particularly long and difficult pirouette near a pillar at the back of the stage and came hurrying down towards him.

He stood for a moment poised on one foot, his eyes closed as he prepared himself for the big moment.

Paddington raised his hat politely once again and then took hold of one of Mr Oblomov's outstretched hands and shook it warmly with his paw.

'Good afternoon, Sir Guy,' he exclaimed. 'I've come to do the *Pas de deux*.'

Sergei Oblomov seemed suddenly to freeze in his position. For a brief moment, in fact, he seemed almost to have turned into stone and Paddington looked at him rather anxiously, but then several things happened to him in quick succession.

First he opened his eyes, then he closed them and a shiver passed through his body, starting at his toes and travelling up to his head, almost as if he had been shot. Then he opened his eyes again and stared distastefully at his hand. It was warm under the lights and some kind of sticky substance seemed to have transferred itself from Paddington's paw.

'It's all right, Sir Guy,' explained Paddington, wiping his paw hastily on one of the folds in his tights. 'It's only marmalade. I forgot to wash it off when I came out of the tuck shop.'

If Mr Oblomov knew what marmalade was or, for that matter, if he'd ever heard of a tuck shop, he gave no sign. A shiver again seemed to pass through his body and as the music reached a crescendo he closed his eyes and with a supreme effort prepared himself once more for the *Pas de deux*.

Feeling very pleased that things seemed to have turned out all right in the end Paddington took hold of Sergei Oblomov's outstretched hand and bent down to pick up his suitcase.

The next moment it felt as if he was in the centre of an earthquake, a tornado and a barrage of thunderbolts all rolled into one.

First it seemed as if his arm had been torn out of its socket, then he felt himself spinning round and round like a top; finally he landed, still spinning, in a heap on

the floor of the stage some distance away from Mr Oblomov.

For a moment he lay where he was gasping for breath and then he struggled to his feet just in time to see a vague figure in tights heading towards him through the glare of the footlights. As he focused on the scene Paddington noticed a nasty looking gleam in Sergei Oblomov's eyes which he didn't like the look of at all and so he hurriedly sat down again.

Mr Oblomov came to a halt and stared down at the figure on the floor. 'I cannot go on,' he exclaimed gloomily. 'For one zing you hov too much shortness – and for zee second thing – your *entrechats* – zey are not clean.'

'My *entrechats* are not clean!' exclaimed Paddington hotly. 'But I had a bath last night.'

'I do not mean zey are dirty,' hissed Mr Oblomov. 'I mean zey should be clean – snappy – like so!'

Without further ado he threw himself into the air, beat his legs together, crossed them in time to the music, and then uncrossed them again as he landed gracefully on one foot facing the audience.

Paddington looked rather doubtful as the applause rang through the hall. 'It's a bit difficult when you've only got paws, Sir Guy,' he exclaimed. 'But I'll have a try.'

Closing his eyes as he'd seen Mr Oblomov do, Paddington jumped into the air, made a half-hearted attempt to cross his legs and then, as his tights began to slip, landed rather heavily on the stage. As he did so, to everyone's surprise he suddenly shot up into the air again, his legs crossing and uncrossing, almost as if he'd been fired from a cannon.

'Good gracious!' exclaimed someone near the Browns, 'that young bear's done a triple!'

'A sixer,' contradicted another elderly gentleman knowledgeably, as Paddington landed and then shot up in the air again with a loud cry. 'Bravo!' he called, trying to make himself heard above the applause.

Even Sergei Oblomov began to look impressed as

Paddington executed several more *entrechats* each one higher and more complicated than the one before. Then, to show he wasn't beaten, he himself gave a tremendous leap into the air, changed his legs over, beat them together, changed them back again, beat them together once more, and then, to a roar from the audience crossed them once again before landing.

Paddington, who had been spending the last few seconds sitting on the stage peering at one of his paws jumped up with a loud cry which echoed round the rafters as Sergei Oblomov landed heavily on his other paw.

If the applause for Sergei Oblomov's *entrechat* had been loud it was nothing compared to that which greeted Paddington as he shot up into the air once more, waving his paws wildly to and fro, crossing and uncrossing them and bringing them together before he landed and then catapulted up again almost out of sight.

This time Sergei Oblomov himself had to acknowledge he'd met his match and with a graceful bow which brought murmurs of approval from the audience he stood back and joined in the applause as the music finally came to an end, and with Paddington's leaps growing higher and wilder with every passing second the curtain came down.

'Well,' said Mr Brown as the applause finally subsided. 'It may not have been the best ballet I've ever seen but but it was certainly the most exciting.'

'Haven't seen anything like it since the Cossacks,' agreed the elderly gentleman near by. 'Five Grand Royales in a row!'

Thoroughly surprised by the events of the afternoon the Browns tried to make their way back stage, but what with the speeches and the crowds of girls who came up to Judy in order to congratulate her on Paddington's performance, it was some while before they were able to force their way through the door at the side of the stage. When they did finally break through they were even more surprised to find that Paddington had been removed to the school sanitorium for what was called 'urgent First Aid.'

'Oh, dear, I hope he hasn't broken anything,' said Mrs Brown anxiously as they hurried across the quadrangle. 'Some of those jumps he did were very high.'

'More likely to have slipped on a marmalade chunk,' said Mrs Bird darkly as they hurried into the ward. But even Mrs Bird looked worried when she caught sight of Paddington lying on a bed with his two back paws sticking up in the air swathed in bandages.

'I can't understand it,' said Miss Grimshaw, as she came forward to greet them. 'Both his back paws are full of holes. I really must find matron and see what she's got to say.'

'Holes?' echoed the Browns.

'Holes,' said Miss Grimshaw. 'Quite small ones. Almost as if he's got woodworm. Not that he could have of course,' she added hastily as a groan came from the direction of the bed.

'Such a shame after the magnificent performance he gave. I doubt if we shall ever see the like again.'

As Miss Grimshaw hurried off in search of the matron Mrs Bird gave a snort. Something about Paddington's leaps on the stage had aroused her suspicions and now her eagle eyes had spotted a number of small shiny objects under the bed that so far no one else had seen.

'Bears who try to pin their tights up with drawing pins,' she said sternly, 'mustn't be surprised when they fall out. And,' she added, 'they mustn't be disappointed if they step on them into the bargain and have to stay in hospital and miss the special marmalade pudding that's waiting for them at home.'

Paddington sat up in bed. 'I think perhaps they're getting better now,' he said hastily.

Being an invalid with everyone fussing around was rather nice. On the other hand, marmalade pudding, particularly Mrs Bird's marmalade pudding, was even nicer.

'But it's no good if you want to carry on dancing,' warned Mrs Bird, as he clambered out of bed and tested his paws on the floor. 'It's much too rich and heavy. In fact, I'm not sure that you oughtn't to go on a diet.'

But Mrs Bird's words fell on empty air as Paddington disappeared through the door in the direction of the car with remarkable haste for one who'd only just risen from a sick bed.

'Perhaps it's as well,' said Mr Brown gravely, as the others followed. 'I can't really picture Paddington embarking on a career as a ballet dancer.'

'All those exercises,' agreed Mrs Brown with a shudder.

'And those tights,' said Judy.

'And all that leaping about,' added Mrs Bird. 'If you ask me it's much better to be simply a bear who likes his marmalade.'

'Especially,' said Jonathan, amid general agreement, 'if you happen to be a bear called Paddington.'

Along Came a Dog

MEINDERT DEJONG

The little red hen was different from all the other hens in the barnyard, and that made her an outcast. She was cocky and mean, but she needed protection. At least that's what the big black dog thought. So he became her slave. He was at the little hen's beck and call. With a swipe of his paw he sent her enemy, the weasel, packing! And a growl drove the squawking rooster away in terror!

He stole eggs from the other hens for her to sit on. Then one day she had five little chicks. The big black dog had a family at last!

Shadrach and *Journey from Peppermint Street* are both Lions. For eight-year-olds and upwards.